VLADICA DJORDJEVIC

You are the Power

CHOOSE TO CREATE THE LIFE YOU DESIRE

AC | P

ACCESS CONSCIOUSNESS PUBLISHING, LLC

You are the Power: Choose to Create the Life You Desire

Published by
Access Consciousness Publishing, LLC
www.accessconsciousnesspublishing.com

Printed in the United States of America

Ease, Joy and Glory

Praise for Vladica Djordjevic

You inspire by telling your "heavy" story, and today you are radiating like the sun itself! One thinks: Who is she? What did she do? As a facilitator, you are present, committed, encouraging and human. I record my conversations with you not to miss all the questions and other things I receive during our meetings. After a mentor meeting with you, I am light, bubbly and enthusiastic! You see and give what I need just in every moment! THANK YOU!

—MALIN SANDELL

You are much more than what you do; you know that your presence is transformation and that your appearance shines on people. Your energy heals, regenerates, raises! Thank you for your unselfish gifts, for teaching me to receive, thanks because I am part of your magic. Always stay so beautiful.

—JELENA CURCIC

I have been coached by Vladica on some occasions and can strongly recommend her skills. After just a few coaching opportunities, I can feel a positive change in my life. Vladica has the ability to support me in the right direction through her intuition, wisdom and experience of working with different people. In addition, I need a coach who dares to be a bit tough and question, and these are qualities that Vladica possesses.

—JENNY ASIMA PERSSON

As a facilitator Vladica is really about more than meets the eye. It is an experience that seems impossible to describe and something you need to try for yourself. Her deep and outstanding knowledge of recovery processes in body, mind and soul is astonishing. This, combined with her profound knowledge of business (20 years professional experience in pioneering diversity in Scandinavia), makes her one of the most versatile facilitators I know!

—ILSE SVENSSON DE JONG

When I met Vladica for the first time, I had just come out of a recent depression, feeling that life could be better than what I had at that time and what I've always had. I told Vladica, "I want to increase my self-esteem," but got so much more, I got a key to managing my own life and my own development, at my own pace, at the same time, free from a bipolar life of alcohol, drugs and sex. For the first time in my conscious life, it had created calm within me. Not only compared to the turmoil I felt before, but a calm I'm not sure is from this reality. I laugh—laugh with ease and without blocks. Life is now like a buffet that is here for me.

—ANONYMOUS

Thank you so much for a nice class, "Letting go by Living NOW," in Copenhagen. Wow, after clearing on how I was a victim in life, it has been much easier to see and be me when I'm feeling manipulated. I almost begin to smile instead of being angry. My son's teachers have begun calling me to tell me how well he is doing in school instead of how hard it is for him. Wow, thanks for the options we have now and what more is possible, what more I can choose.

—KAREN

Vladica is a woman who inspires many people, by her example, to continue their lives, despite the fact that those lives brought pain. Her power and capacity radiate as a great light and send a clear message—everything is possible when we have awareness about our choices. Choosing yourself is a brave and courageous decision, and it is possible if we have consciousness of what is possible! This book is a GIFT for all of us who hold it in our hands.

Thank you.

—JELENA MILANOVIĆ, AUTHOR OF *CHOOSE YOURSELF*

I believe that the life of any person who reaches the last page of this book will never be the same again. These pages contain an incredible life, a script that could only be written by a great expert. So much grief, so much despair, but also love and joy, completes every sentence.

It takes great courage to expose yourself completely, to "get out" of your life and see it as an observer and give it the opportunity to appear in some other way—on the pages of a book. At first glance it is only devoted to a terrible event. In essence, the book is dedicated to life and its glory that never disappears.

—JASMINA STEFANOVIĆ

Vladica's life journey is a great inspiration to all who chose to move on after difficult situations in life. Her strength, energy and joy of life are contagious. Her compassion and ability to feel other people is a huge contribution.

I am grateful that I am part of her journey.

—MIA LARSSON, PROFESSOR, SWEDEN

I'm beyond grateful for my mother and blessed to be able to call her my best friend, mentor and biggest supporter. My mom is one of the strongest women I know, and every day she inspires me to see possibilities and step into my true potency. Every day she provides unconditional support and love, regardless of how busy she is or what hardship she's going through. Our lives have not been easy, with countless traumatic events, including abusive family members, my brother's drug abuse and murder. However, life is not what happens to you, it's what you create.

All of the hardships that we've endured and overcome have made us both stronger and who we are today. All of our hardships have been gifts. Our past experiences and the learnings they've brought have enabled my mother to contribute and help countless of people around the world, including myself. Thank you mom for the gift that you are! I hope everyone who reads this book becomes inspired and learns from it, just like I do every single day by being around my mother.

—ALEXANDRA IVANCEVIC

With gratitude

Oh, boy!

It is easy to express gratitude when you know that every single being on planet Earth is connected to and contributes to the life form of this book. The planet itself asked me to write it. The trees, the plants, the animals asked me to share, to touch, and to make a difference.

I'd like to start by thanking *me* for my choices and for my willingness, patience and stubbornness to step into the capacities, gifts, and abilities I have and for choosing to be the catalyzer and make a difference.

Now, I am full of wonder! My first questions to you are:

What would it take for you to be inspired to choose *you*?

What choices can you make to step into your capacities and play with the abilities and talents you already have?

Do you know that *you* have all the choices possible? The ones that create limitations and the ones that create expansion. The ones that create grief and the ones that create joy. What if we get the contribution we can be to the Earth by *every choice* we make! Would that awareness create a different possibility? Our energy is what *creates*! The question is what energy are you *willing to be*?

I´d like to thank the editor of the version of this book, originally published in Serbia and Croatia, Jasmina Stefanovic, for her ability to tap into my history and be present with the energy. A beautiful being—humble, sweet, potent and very patient with me and the intense energy I am. I fried her brain the first three days working together on the book, but she didn't stop being present for me. She listened carefully to everything I talked about with no judgment and opened up to receive me in totality.

I would also like to express my gratitude to Mia Larsson, a professor from Sweden, who asked me a few years ago to write my story and to give it life. She was always saying, "Vladi you have to get this book out..." She was the first to read my story and help shape it into what it is today.

People ask me: *How did you do it? What did you do to move on and make it work? Please let us know! The world needs your story!* This inspired me to start writing.

It is amazing how people show up in your life when you accept the power of manifestation, of asking and receiving with gratitude. I was asking, *who can I find to edit the English version of this book?*

One day while I was visiting my daughter Alexandra in New York City, she introduced me to her colleague, Jami Kelmenson, with whom I immediately felt an energetic connection. Later on, my daughter said, "Mom why don't you ask Jami to edit your book? She is an amazing writer!"

Yes, she is. The story touched her heart, and she touched mine by her willingness to lend her talents and motivation to help this book reach a U.S. and global audience. Huge gratitude for her enthusiasm and being "us" all the way to get it published.

With tremendous gratitude to my children, especially my son Ivan, who was killed on Midsummer Eve, the most festive night of the year in Sweden. I am so grateful that he chose me to be his mom, for sharing 30 years with me, and for teaching me that we are just conscious instruments of God.

HUGE Gratitude to my amazing, conscious daughter, Alexandra, for being the Light that lights the dark, for her willingness to always choose and be greater each day, and for her unconditional love to stay by my side no matter what.

Gratitude to hundreds of people including my parents, friends, teachers, enemies, gurus—everyone, and everybody that I have and haven't mentioned in this book who, in this reality and non-reality, gifted me the key to unlock every limitation I bought as true and real.

I´d like to thank you mothers, fathers, women, men, children attending my classes for your gratitude and for inspiring me to write.

Gratitude to all the teachings and tools from leadership trainings, yoga philosophy, homeopathy, FIRO Theory (Fundamental Interpersonal Relationship Orientation) and Access Consciousness.

One year before the death of my son, I found the tools of Access Consciousness that contributed to my choices. I became an Access Consciousness facilitator and have been teaching the tools and techniques all around the world to thousands of people. Tools that allow you to change anything you cannot change and to create everything you desire in a different and easier way. Tools that make me laugh and give me a totally different perspective on life.

By facilitating and contributing to people, my life is expanding and changing. The moment I chose gratitude, everything changed. Thank YOU.

Huge thank you to the the founders of Access Consciousness, Gary Douglas and Dr. Dain Heer, for gifting me tools, and the energy to move from surviving to thriving. Their allowance and empowerment on my journey is beyond words.

Huge thank you to all my colleagues all around the world for their caring, loving, and nurturing energy and to all my hosts and organizers.

Thank you to YOU reading this book. Somehow it found its way to your hands. Are you willing to step into your capacities, gifts, talents and abilities?

What would it take for this book to be the traveller that reaches everyone that needs inspiration?

What would it take for this book to be in every home and be read by millions of people? What would it take for this book to be the seed planted in your head to create your life, for choosing life, for ease and joy and glory and for being a contribution to your life and to Mother Earth?

What would living look like then?

With gratitude,
Vladica

To my son Ivan,
for showing up everywhere in other bodies
and being stubborn enough to get my attention,
so that I understand that
death doesn't exist.

Contents

Part IV: Coaching and Meditations

Coaching   **112**

Meditations

*Nothing should shake you
from the awakening art that is within you:
the art of living and the art of being you.*

VLADICA DJORDJEVIC

A calling to tell my story

Welcome to the power of YOU.

This book is many things, but mostly it is a calling to tell my story. It is not a guarantee that if you do what I did, and follow the tools presented here, that you will live life with the ease and joy that I do. But it is an invitation to consider the possibilities and acknowledge that there can be another way for you to choose to live—to be happy—no matter the circumstances you are currently facing.

I made the choice to tell my story to give it life, to travel the world and have it translated into many languages, because the gift that my son Ivan gave me is a universal one. My choice is to devote the rest of my life to giving you, the reader, a different possibility. I choose to give you hope, inspiration and motivation with my story and the tools I used to change my life—the tools that helped me survive when murder invaded eight years ago, and the same tools that I use on a daily basis to move on, thrive and make a difference in the world.

The manner in which I embraced life after the brutal murder of my son Ivan was met with a range of emotions from people in my world—admiration, inspiration, confusion, judgment, resistance and, most often, looming questions: *How did she do it? Why did she choose this way? What is her secret?*

Noticing the choices I made after the devastating event, people sent me messages asking for advice about their own situations and also to express gratitude and appreciation. Their willingness to reach out inspired me to contribute even more. It was then that this book asked to be born.

I wrote this book to honor my son and his choice and to offer this possibility: that death is NOT the end of life, and life is not the beginning. Ivan's life and death made a difference, and he was/ is valuable, as are we all. It is my intention through this book to demonstrate that each one of us is a Gift to the world. The planet requires your energy. There is no beginning and no end. Everything is here, right now, in one form or another.

Through these words, I hope to encourage you to realize that life is life, life will move, life will be lived, and life is not more powerful than you. Your choices are what creates your life, and I wrote this book to empower you to choose YOU, no matter what. My choice is to be totally naked in my vulnerability and to show you a different possibility.

You, my friend, have talents, abilities and capacities that you can discover through the choices you make. Are you willing to become more creative, more productive, have more ideas instead of sitting in your stuff and letting that be your conclusion? Are you willing to to find your choice?

Then this book is dedicated to YOU.

You might be suffering or have lost hope. You may be experiencing financial or relationship problems—these are your problems, not your life. You may have been born with more money than you need, but are still unable to be happy. This book is for you, too.

What if happiness has nothing to do with what you think it does? What if, instead of focusing on your problems so intently, you chose to focus on the opportunities inspired by creation that are available to you all the time? What would you choose then? Where would you be? Who would you be? Knowing with certainty that there is something else possible for you and your loved ones is the first step toward discovering what that means for you. In the ten seconds it took you to read that sentence, you could have made the choice to find out what that is.

So, this book is for those of you who want to be happy and want the inspiration to choose happiness—and I mean REALLY happy—so happy that others will desire to have what you have!

One day five years ago, a woman came to one of my workshops. I knew this woman, and I asked her: "Why are you here?" Her answer was: "I am not here because of this class; I don't know what this class is all about. I have everything I require in life: marriage, children, a large successful company, travel, and friends. But you have something that I don't have. I've been watching you over the years, and I know your story. I've seen you change, the lightness and the sparkle that you are spreading around you, that is what I want."

By way of this story I would like to ask you: When did you forget that you are the spark and the force that lights the world? It is something we are all born with, but we make the choice to forget where we came from. I made a conscious choice eight years ago—I chose life, here and now, despite all the chaos that was occurring around me, and I chose to discard, in the moment, that which I knew was not working for me.

Before making this choice, I would sit with my friends talking…
and talking— lamenting all of our problems, in detail, coming
up with so many conclusions and solutions, none of which ever
solved anything. Does this sound familiar?

Now, instead of talking, I act in the moment I become fully aware
of the situation. In that moment, I make a choice as to how I
want to change things. I receive the awareness through asking
questions and trusting my ability to know what is light, fun and
easy. Choosing light and fun *always* opens up more possibilities
than wading in the dirt and heaviness of problems. What if that
which you are making so dirty and awful, has a beauty that you
are not willing to receive just because you have decided that it is a
problem? Are problems really real?

I have discovered through my journey that our problems are our
way of living life so that we always have something to overcome
and so that we can justify the choices we have already made.
Wouldn't it be more fun if we were free from the need to justify
our positions and make another choice?

Choosing "lightness" and "sparkle" allows us to see all the beauty
in life. After I made my choice, which led to some surprising
changes, I increasingly saw the beauty in the small things in
life—the velvety redness of a rose, the strength of a beggar to
sit in the rain looking for a handout, the richness in simplicity.
I also realized how easily I could change things—from anger to
peace, from lament to creation, from dis-ease in my body to ease
in my body, from spending money to creating money, from pain
to painless, from lack and need to abundance. It is just a choice.

This book is dedicated to you who have suffered enough in your
own unconsciousness born of a reality that convinces us there are
limits and that you cannot have it all, be more or be it all. It is time
for all of us to become MASTERS and to live in true freedom.

It is time to be the Source. This is not the birthright of only a few people. It is for everyone! It is about rising above your mind's chatter and honing the awareness—the consciousness—that is already within you.

Welcome to the journey of YOU embracing different possibilities and stepping into the magic of who you REALLY are. Are you ready to experience the miracle of what we call life and the great human capacity to go beyond yourself, to jump out of what you believe to be your problems, to climb to different levels of your life just to see what's there? Let´s go!!! Let´s walk, play and plant seeds on the golden field of consciousness. ARE YOU READY? Are you ready to laugh, to cry, to scream, to enjoy, and to change and let go of every limitation keeping you from living totally, joyfully, happy now and forever? Amen!

No matter what your life looks like now, no matter what's going on for you, if any of my words have resonated thus far, please continue with my story. If you choose to close this book now, I wish you peace, happiness and good choices always. But I will leave you with this—what would it take for us to meet one day? Just one possibility of many that I hope will come to fruition.

Thank You.

How to read this book

Parts I and II of this book are devoted to the love story I shared with my son Ivan. I share these intimate details not to brag or make you feel sorry for me, but to demonstrate the act of resilience and thriving. My story is not a happy one, but the choices it led me to have resulted in some of the happiest days of my life—with many more yet to come; of this I am certain.

Part III reflects on some common themes in life. Opening ourselves up to different choices can create some astounding outcomes.

Interwoven into my story are coaching signals that will lead you to the words I might use in my workshops when I am working with someone related to the topic addressed in my story. Quite simply, if something in my story resonates with you, and there is a signal to "See Coaching and Meditations, p. X", this means you might want to turn ahead to Part IV of this book and find some wisdom in the words I share there. Or, you can read the book in order and gather all the coaching wisdom in at once! It is your choice.

Chapter **One**

A child's deeper knowledge

Self-knowledge is best learned not by contemplation,
but by action. Strive to do your duty, and you will
soon discover what stuff you are made of.

—JOHAN GOETHE

I felt the touch like a gentle wind. The darkness hid everything else.
And then, through that black density, the voice, quiet and gentle, broke
through, as if floating in the room:

"You're 'special,'" it said.

I jumped, startled, because I know it's that part of the night where
all is unearthly quiet, everyone asleep, and outside the window—just
blackness. The night was surrounding everything...but where does this
voice come from? Maybe a dream?

I'm convinced it was real. A touch and a voice woke me that night, no matter how impossible it seemed.

In the morning, I told everything to my Grandma. In the first few moments, she looked at me quizzically, but then the penetrating face, wrapped in a colorful scarf, gently smiled and said:

"Vladica, it was just a dream, even though I know you're a special girl, especially for me. Come on now, have breakfast, and go to the snow."

Her voice seemed totally carefree, but as I was leaving, I felt a glance follow me as I dashed through the door.

I ran outside as if I were flying out of the house, rejoicing in the new day, which hinted at the unusual, beautiful winter idyll cradling our small town. I was thinking of how I could use this day in the best way possible to have fun and to gather lots of children from the neighborhood around me, a community celebration of what, I wasn't quite sure.

But I was the leader. And that seemed completely natural to me.

Cheerful faces awaited in their warm homes, behind blurred windows. They were ready for my small figure loaded with a vortex of energy to make the first steps on the white carpet that was woven during the night. Suddenly the doors of the surrounding houses began to open, and "my students" started running outside. Imitating our strict school teacher, I rigidly straightened my back, frowned and said, authoritatively:

"You are late!"

At that moment, we all burst into a thunderous laugh that spread through the air, mingling with the smell of winter. Like a teacher at school, with a thin stick in my hand, I knew my task was to explain to the neighborhood children how to "live a life," as though foreshadowing the collective knowledge of the world archived for centuries, eons even, in all of the libraries of the Universe.

There was so much joy! The kind of joy I could rarely catch in later years, even when many things were conspiring to make me as happy as soft silk.

At the moment when this memory first begins, when I first heard the voice, I was ten years old and lived with my grandmother in a small house in the eastern part of Serbia, in a place that does not exist on any map. From ancient times, it was believed that in this region lived wizard women with special powers. Mysticism and magic were part of our everyday life, an indispensable part of my growing up.

In the past eight years, I have learned to fear nothing. And this absence of fear, replaced with only the purest acceptance of joy hinted at on that day half a century ago, served to me as if on a plate, created a completely different projection of my reality. This is the reality in which I transmitted "my knowledge"—which I am sure is my gift to share.

The other side of my young being in that mystical village was completely wild. Everyone knew me as the "barefoot girl," who went out without shoes, even in the snow. My home was a place only for sleeping and eating (my home in recent years has almost the same function—a coincidence?!). I lived in the infinity of my freedom. I visited people around the village, visited houses to "talk" a little, and "spread my ideas," which were especially interesting for adults. Interesting for everybody, except for my parents, who sometimes couldn't find me for hours.

Grandma often used to say:

"I wonder what kind of future this child will have!? She's so different!" (If she only knew!)

My parents weren't happy about what I see now as my calling. They kept repeating the phrases that the child's heart "filled with mischief" should heed:

"Be good."

"Do not make trouble."

"Why aren't you like the other girls?!" (Why am I not? That's a really good question.)

I was the only girl in the Djordjevic family, and therefore I'd had special status since my birth. This is like a golden thread that runs through my entire life, because the behavior of my close relatives, even after several decades, has not changed toward me. Even today, I am still a little girl who cried for three days because my cousin Krsto married.

I was intent on going with him and his wife Bosa on their honeymoon, curious to understand more about and seek evidence of their love. I did not get what I wanted. I was 14-years-old and in a complete euphoria of feelings, beautiful, overwhelming, but for me also sad. Krsta wanted to somehow soothe me. However, there was someone reasonable in their new union who would not allow a young lovestruck girl to intrude upon the beginning of a common life.

While my parents yearned for a better and easier life than what the economy of Serbia offered, several of us lived as one family for the first ten years of my life. Three Djordjevic houses were crammed together next to one another: in one—my parents, grandmother and me; in the others, Krsta and Bosa, and a few other cousins.

Most of their attention was directed toward me when I arrived on September 14, 1960. Dad behaved like a goddess had been born. That adoration was mutual. I used to say that when I grew up, I would find a man like him—entertaining, handsome, merry. These are the parts of his character that were passed down to me. I still recognize him as the second being in the mirror, always there, always a part of me.

With his cheerful smile and boundless joy, my father's spirit shined on my childhood days. It was different with my mother. She played her life role as a victim so well that she did not give anyone the space to get close to her. Not my father, not me. For her, love was expressed in a completely different way, which, in that early childhood, I could not even understand or accept. It is incredible, however, that, regardless of my innate wisdom of understanding my mother's detachment, I have chosen to copy her behavior toward men in my own life.

Isn't it time for me to make a different choice?

People from different parts of the country would come in secret to see into the future through a conversation with a woman who was said to have special powers, or could contact someone from the other world. (Back in Serbia, we did not know anything about the magic of consciousness, or psychic abilities, at least on any academic level.) We listened to those stories and often used magic words in play, invoked fairies and ghosts, experiencing them as part of our reality. We believed in fairy tales, in magic, that the Earth was talking to us. We communicated in a language that was a combination of Romanian, Serbian, Italian, and God knows what else. The newcomers mostly did not understand us. They could not learn our language at any university. Perhaps, for them, our world was even weirder.

See Coaching and Meditations: "The magic of consciousness," p. 112

We also listened to the stories that the elders told us about the two big wars that had stormed the area and taken many lives. The remaining survivors mourned, and in their own way, used the knowledge they had channeled from their ancestors about how to enter the other worlds and see those who no longer existed in the current reality. Often these worlds were tied together in the stories, so we were not always sure of the end of one, or the beginning of another. Mostly, we were interested in romantic stories about love and passion, and we poked each other and laughed and smiled as we listened to them. Although it seemed like something that would never happen to us, we secretly dreamed about it, especially the girls.

In winter, we would gather around a fire in one of the children's houses, and during the summer, we would meet every night around a big tree in my aunt's garden. Although I had not yet stepped into the second decade of my life, sometimes it was inconceivable for me not to talk about events from the past, attaching so much importance to things that remained in other times. A time when brave people who knew all about nature talked to it as though with a neighbor. And appreciated every sign that it would send them.

When you live on the border of the two worlds, you discover that the borders actually do not exist.

The connection with Mother Earth and nature was something that was a matter of course in my childhood. Sickness was treated with natural means. I recall that the best cure for my temperature was a sock soaked in brandy or vinegar diluted with water, and sometimes I would tie a scarf filled with fresh potatoes around my head. And the next day I'd be healthy.

Mother Earth had a solution for everything.

We are all her children, and we got so many benefits from Her, but we forgot to use them. Often, they would look like magic, and magic is essentially nature itself. In ancient times, this connection between the living beings and Mother Earth was much stronger and took place with little opposition. In the part of the planet in which I grew up, more so than many other places that tout their inherent spiritual foundations through water, or air or earth today, this connection was especially evident.

Gary Douglas, founder of Access Consciousness, expresses the potency of nature as follows:

> Communion is that which nature is, communion is that which Oneness is. You have always the awareness of that when you go out in nature, now why don't you bring nature in to you? Become the embodiment of all that nature is and see who speaks to you. The plants, the animals, the houses, the chairs, the cars, the furniture, the floors, the ceiling, all will speak. You have heard the expression that walls can speak, they can, you just don't listen. The plants have language, so do the animals, it is not the verbal garbage and diarrhea that you are used to, but it is succinct and clear if you will listen.

The cloak of my fairytale childhood was torn as though by a knife through a single event, setting my calm river ablaze. My parents decided to move to Austria, then to Germany, and finally to the far north—to Sweden—without me. I felt betrayed, mostly by my beloved father. The brightness of my childhood, which I illuminated as a reflector, almost disappeared completely.

☞ *See Coaching and Meditations, "Conflict lines", p. 114*

When my mom and dad left, my grandmother devoted her life to me completely. I constantly felt the warmth of that colorful scarf knitted with boundless tones of love. She was not one of those ordinary grandmothers, thinking only about what we would eat and what we would wear, how to be a better student, and so on. She was a stable pillar, which, in my first steps towards the life I would soon come to know, I counted on to support me in becoming me, finding my authentic self, even when it was completely unrecognizable to anyone else.

"Always follow your dreams, do not let anyone disturb them," she'd say to me while peeling potatoes for dinner and enjoying the sunset, relaxed after all the day's tasks.

I would then look at her and nod assuredly, as if I understood exactly what she meant. And no matter how mysterious her words sounded to me, not fully comprehending what she was talking about…I told her my dreams. I understood then that no one could disturb what I've already dreamed, and so in the fog of her words, I somehow felt their importance, as transcendent messages that should be placed in a box to one day confidently open and understand their meaning.

My grandmother constantly led me to fields soaked in sunlight. There was a time when clovers were collected, mostly during wheat and corn seasons. The villagers produce what they need during the hot months and prepare for the winter snows, whose white coating hides the boundaries between properties.

In that time and place, neighbors helped each other as a large family. There was a sense of community that probably only exists today in rare corners of our planet. There was no technology, cars, motors or television, and yet there was so much happiness and joy when the plants—which nature gives unconditionally after sowing—appeared from the Earth. I remember that I had eaten the sweetest tomato straight from my grandfather's hat, one he had picked up somewhere in the field.

During the cold days, we would go to sleep with first sign of darkness. The only thing that could disperse the darkness was the light of the candles that stood as guards at the dining table so we could briefly enjoy the winter's feast of vegetables we had picked. Another source of light, but also warmth, which brought a special sense of peace to the room, was the one that spread from the wood stove, the crackling of which lulled us to sleep. Grandma and I slept in the same room.

Recalling that time, I can almost feel the breath and warmth of her body. The energy she emitted from every part of her being on those long, cold nights brought warmth in the form of security, dedication and joy. I can invite in that feeling any time I need calmness. She was illiterate, but the wisest and bravest woman I have ever known. Her reactions were often quite different from what I would have expected, as if a deeper knowing lay within her. She was the perfect model for a girl who grew up freely and unburdened and in symbiosis with the cosmic forces that surrounded her.

I remember an event when she showed her truth.

Snow was falling, gold fire torches danced in a warm oven, food was waiting on the table—a typical scene in our home. I looked up at the curtained face, trying to figure out how to explain to my "wall", the pillar of my life, what had happened. Stuttering and searching for words that would come out as smoothly as possible, I tangled the message as I looked down at the floor instead of into her eyes. I explained how I had lost the coins she had given me. I had kept them tied in a colorful handkerchief, playing, throwing it high in the air as I jumped in the snow. At one point, the handkerchief opened and the gold discs fluttered as drops of water in all directions. There was no way I could find them, no matter how much I dug into the deep snow. I knew how much each coin meant to us and that they were not toys to be played with, but now I had only one choice—to admit what happened. The answer I received was not the one I expected. Grandma calmly said:

"Why are you worried? As long as we have each other, we have everything. With a piece of bread and food on the table, we are rich. We are healthy and have each other. We're the richest people in the world. And when the snow melts, the coins will be waiting for us in front of the house. And even if they aren't, there will be new ones. Money is not important, we are! As long as we have our hands and our magic, we will get anything we ask for."

For the first time, I understood that there is a different perspective on wealth.

Life seemed so exciting to me.

☞ *See Coaching and Meditations, "The powerlessness of money," p. 114*

Chapter *Two*

A strange girl in a foreign land

Today I still seek ways to infuse the pure joy I felt in my early childhood into my view of money, and my life. We are creatures of joy and ease.

My first doll was made of corn. She had yellow hair and green clothes, and for a long time I was convinced that she was the most beautiful doll in the world. I dressed her in small sundries, some pieces of cloth. I always had serious conversations with her.

Once I told her something that I could not say even to my grandma, because I didn't want to see a trace of grief line her beautiful face. So, I talked with the doll:

"I do not know why they left me. But, don't worry, I'm happy to have you, and all of my companions and friends, and grandma...

but I miss them. How is it possible that they do not miss me? Other parents are with their children; they do not leave them with their grandmother and go to a distant world. And they come back so rarely. Well, they will not recognize me when they see me the next time. They had to go to that Sweden to work. As if there were no jobs here? And there are no people like our neighbors there. Certainly nobody as nice. And who knows what they do there at all? I cannot understand it, and I'm often mad at them. You understand me, don't you?"

I would look down at the doll, waiting for her confirmation that I was right. And I was, indeed.

One day they came back, and my anger toward them shifted, just a bit.

They brought gifts. I'd never seen so many great and beautiful things before. I was completely fascinated and absorbed with every word they said about life in Sweden—*everything is modern, you can earn a lot of money, life is easier, they do not have to work in the fields...* I wanted to go with them, so I, their child, could feel the charms of the Promised Land. But their answer was cruel:

"No! You stay here with your grandmother!"

"Alright then, if you do not bring me with you, I will kill myself," I threatened.

And it sounds almost incredible, looking back, but they believed my words and decided to bring me with them.

I came to Sweden where I had everything I wanted, except that I lost something.

I lost myself.

☞ *See Coaching and Meditations, "Saving yourself," p. 117*

Two months before I started writing this book, my mom passed away. In recent years, she had lived in the place where I spent the first decade of my life. A few sunny summer days of seeing her gave me a chance to visit all the favorite places from my childhood.

Each day started with a long walk by the Danube, which now did not look as large and as powerful as in my childhood, but I felt that I was welcome in that place. As it always was, nature was generous. Such a scent of flowers does not exist everywhere. Or, maybe it just smells like my childhood and wants to remind me of the carefree days that ended when I went to live in another country. Looking at the dance of butterflies in the endless field of color and beauty, I could not catch my breath because of the emotions that brought me back into the past. Here my fortune grew; here I was bathed with joy, running barefoot, absorbing the energy of the Earth, living in constant connection with it. Nature gave me strength and taught me what is really important.

Nevertheless, I wanted to leave at that time. We always think we need more. And luck is modest. If we do not see it, it only disappoints—and leaves.

This is how it was for my parents, a couple who could not live with or without each other. The word "happiness" was not in their vocabulary, and I accepted that as a reality in my childhood.

Growing up with them in Sweden, I forgot who I was, what my purpose was. I forgot my skills, my potential, my strength, and my joy! I remember constantly thinking: "Something is missing here!"

That was when I completely separated from myself. And many times it occurred to me that something was wrong with me, that some part of me, an important part, got lost somewhere. Gone! And at some point, I decided to find and reclaim it.

The memories gathered around me on that warm, lazy day as I walked along the river. Life was so simple and relaxed before I left this place. And everything was lasting. I often played with lambs in my grandmother's room because they were allowed to enter our home. I washed my hair with rainwater my grandmother collected in special pots, bathing in a small wash bucket, because at that time we had no bathtub.

If I wanted chocolate, my grandmother would give me an egg— an oval white treasure provided to us one morning by one of the colorful chickens in the yard, and I, proudly holding it in my hand, ran to the store. The vendor would take the egg, and in return give me a chocolate bar. Oh, how fantastic it was! One fair exchange of things we both wanted.

The smile returned to my face because the memories came as though being called from a megaphone. I walked the path that I often wandered, running with a stick in my hand that I was convinced was magical, that it was enough for me to make a wish and swing it, and everything would come true. All people are happy, and there is no end. What happened? Where did all this go?

Sweden.

My first encounter with the country I so longed to call home was gloomy. It was raining, and that grayness made me feel totally helpless. My first encounter with school was even worse. I woke up late, which caused my mother to react with a real outburst of anger.

"Wake up! You have to go to school! You have to take care of yourself! Get up fast!"

She hit me with a brush furiously. It did not take much time for me to realize that she was always angry. This was what our communication often looked like.

I often thought that if I ever had children, I would never be like her. Never! Who is this evil woman? My mother? Impossible—everything inside me was screaming, while I was trying to figure out at what point someone replaced my mother with this witch.

Terrible things were happening, one after the other. In school, I was the only student from another country, and everyone looked at me with such undignified interest, as if I had just arrived at a zoo from a distant, exotic country. I did not know how to speak their language. I did not understand them. My clothes were different from theirs, and it looked like someone dropped me down from the sky to another planet, took me by the hand and just placed me somewhere far away. Make that, *threw* me.

My father did not allow me to wear my beautiful, long golden hair, because, he said:

"Good girls do not look like savages."

My lovely, admired dad scared me at those moments. I was also scared at school. I had to do something, take things into my own hands and change this. I did not have to live like this. I could not replace my parents...so, what am I supposed to do?

Well, I chose to fight with the boys. And after that, they became my friends. The next thing that brought me popularity was dance. No one could dance the Russian carousel better than me. It's a dance of jumping and rotating in a circle. Or the traditional dance from my country, called *Vlajna*. I was skillful; everything I learned about life from nature, I could use. So, I did it, with my body and my mind.

I was ten years old, living in a new country, with new friends and constantly angry parents. So, I became a very angry girl myself.

☞ *See Coaching and Meditations, "What is anger?" p. 118*

Our impossible shared life could no longer go on. So what did my parents do? They brought my stable, "rock" grandmother to Sweden. It is interesting that I remember very little before her arrival, as if I lived in a state of delirium.

The arrival of the oldest family member made everyday life easier for us. My parents worked—a lot; my grandmother took care of the house and me, and we spent five weeks in Serbia every year for holiday, in our fairytale village. The circle was turning.

The life mission of most Serbians, who go abroad (the so-called "gastarbajter"), is to build a house—bigger and better than the one in the village you left and to return one day and finally enjoy the "goods" that you had created, even if this was achieved in a most difficult way and without joy. To show other people how much you've done, there in the distant world. To find happiness through material things.

And what is the point?

☞ *See Coaching and Meditations, "Projections and expectations," p. 119*

For several years, with my family in Sweden, our common time together would appear idyllic. But the reality I lived in did not reveal itself to the outside world. The time my mother spent on this planet was devoted to my father and her unconditional love for him, wanting to be the only one he would ever look at with eyes full of worship. And she was never satisfied.

Years later, I asked her:

"Is there anything in your life that makes you happy?"

Before the answer came, I felt it in the air.

"No, my life is just suffering."

"What about me? You also have grandchildren. Haven't we brought joy to your life?"

"Well, you're here. What's your question? You cannot bring me joy only because of your existence. You're just here, that's a fact."

For my mother, we were nothing more than decorative flowers in the room. At least that's what I thought. The constant complaining, regret, anger and rage with which she lived were slowly destroying her life force. The role of the victim she had proudly played was immovable. It is fascinating how we manage to create our inner world where pain and suffering are so strong that there is no room for anything else.

☞ *See Coaching and Meditations, "How do we defend ourselves against fear?" p. 121*

Our memories reflect our subjective assessments of what has happened to us. After my mother's death, my father has yet to come to grips with being alone, and keeps telling the story about my mom as the love of his life. It seems as though I lived in a parallel world when he speaks of her as dear, good, always there for him and always accepting of who he is. Dad is even more unhappy now because he misses what they had. Their arguments represented love for them, because love has many dimensions, and this was their expression.

Perhaps when some people are no longer with us in this reality, our reality about them begins to change.

A few years ago, I asked my father:

"Is there anything I can do for you to make you happy?"

His honest answer was:

"Why are you trying? I enjoy being poor! Go and live your life and let me live the way I want to."

When my mother was old and sick, all my convictions disappeared, and I could see her fear, her love, her humility, and joy that she never showed. She gave too much importance to other people and their thoughts, thereby limiting herself.

She became the victim of her choices.

☞ *See Coaching and Meditations, "Learning to choose," p. 122*

I still remember quite clearly, as if the past walked into the room I am standing in now, the desire for my parents and I to love each other without arguing, without tension. I tried with all the knowledge a child could have, to understand their behavior, but as a result, from an early age, I was not present in my body. Getting out of my own body was the easiest way to avoid pain.

Sometimes I did not talk to them for days because I could not listen to them quarreling. In my fantasies, I created a divine life in which a prince appears—that wonderful being, a person worthy of trust that will save me. Save me from myself.

So, I waited, and waited, and waited. And I "kissed the frogs."

If somebody had told me then that the only person who could save me was walking with me every day—that the savior was me—I would have thought they were on their way to a madhouse.

I, only I, can save myself.

And the only person who is always there for you—is you. The only person who really knows you—is you. How much longer will you run away from your strength? Where will you run to? Unfortunately, you cannot escape because reality knocks on your door with various surprises, guaranteed.

At that time, I did not understand this.

Days were passing as though on an endless track, life was happening, and I did not even "touch" it. Everything was hard, and there was no joy anywhere. Waiting for someone to rescue me would take too long, and there was never any sign appearing to indicate that "they" were coming or that anything would change.

At the age of 17, I decided to marry. That seemed to me the only way to find myself.

I married and created with my husband the same relationship that my parents had.

See Coaching and Meditations, "Responsibility for our reality," p. 123

PART II

Ivan – The Gift

A NEW BEGINNING

THE FIRST LOSS

WHEN MURDER INVADES

Chapter *Three*

A new beginning

It's your choice, NOT your upbringing that creates your reality.

—DAIN HEER

It was snowing outside, although it was the second half of April. But what was happening outside was completely irrelevant at the moment, because a beautiful being was sleeping in my arms. What a gift! The gift that cannot be measured with anything else that life can send us. With his eyes closed, in a state of complete bliss and peace, my son was sleeping.

I did not plan to become a mother and, honestly, I had no idea what it all meant. If I could have suspected how much vulnerability it would bring, the level of awareness, I would certainly have considered whether I was ready for such a role at that time.

Meeting the man who was to become my husband, the father of this sleeping gift, was like a scene from a movie. Maybe this excitement completely interferes with us being able to see another side of reality. But isn't it like that for all of us? When you fall in love, it feels like another dimension to life, as if everything around the two of you is there because of your love, especially if you are as young as we were.

I was convinced that something was wrong with me, and so I went to the doctor. He was accustomed to sharing such news with immense joy, so with a pleased face, he said:

"My dear, nothing is wrong with you. You're in the third month of pregnancy."

Today I believe that in the fascinating moment of creation, Ivan chose us as parents for his life journey on this planet. I also believe that none of us lives only one life, but that our lives are changing and that we take on different roles: from the poor to the rich—anything that we need to complete our experience and erase the various vows we have with people. We are all here to reach our consciousness.

☞ *See Coaching and Meditations: "When do we become consciousness?," p. 124*

Still not knowing about the news, my future husband decided to move us from Serbia to Sweden, that Promised Land, especially for those of us who lived poorly in Serbia. Though surrounded by greenery and the brightness of the sun, we were insufficiently inspired toward any progress.

When the train finally arrived at the station—where people of many different nations were waiting alongside us with a sparkling glow in their eyes, as though expecting somebody dear and important—I shouted out so loudly that our fellow travelers, despite their own excitement, turned in search of my voice:

"We're going to be parents!"

To my youthful exuberance, my husband's shiny face was sufficient proof of his love, which we would share with a being to join us on the planet six months later.

However, the love that began in quite different circumstances in Serbia, in a completely carefree craze for each other, hardly found its way to our new beginning. Relations between us had sometimes reached a high intensity, as if the Universe was deliberately playing with us, testing the limits of patience in our restless, young souls.

When we arrived in Sweden, my husband worked at a factory where the rules were rigid. A totally different life than he had before in Serbia, one filled with obligations and responsibilities, did not make him happy. In that period, we decided to move in with my grandmother, to save some money. At first, this seemed like a reasonable decision, but it didn't prove to be the best solution.

Everyday frustrations and dissatisfactions melted our feelings like flames. Unfortunately, it was a way of life that was not unknown to me, and it did not surprise me much. I didn't know that there could be something better, because I did not have an example. It was the same relationship that had existed for years between my parents, so I just took over their story, no matter how much I wanted to get away and create something different.

My son came into this world of chaos and drama. The day the miracle happened was April 19th—a great miracle, indeed, for a young mom. I laughed loudly as if I wanted the whole Universe to hear me, and cried at the same time with more joy than I had ever felt in my life.

My eyes only saw this tiny creature that was part of my being, now separate. I was completely amazed. I couldn't possibly comprehend at that point that our future would be so terrible. The power and potential that we would develop and expand through joy were taken by a demonic energy that grabbed our lives with claws, controlling it completely. Instead, something completely different happened. Something that wasn't an option even in the worst nightmares.

The first days were like a dream. I walked, talked, ate, but it was as if none of that really existed. Blinded with so much beauty, I sat for hours and watched my baby's little fingers and feet, tilted over him to check if he was breathing, without blinking, staring at this unreal creature that was mine.

I was a young mother, barely two decades into my existence, and I already given a new life to the world. I tried to make up for my inexperience by reading everything I could find about baby care—what is good, what is not—whether I had put the baby to sleep properly, whether he was hungry, what the signals I got from him meant. I followed the rules and instructions of various experts like an alert student from the first bench, but it seemed to me that it did not help much. It was not easy to raise another being, and perhaps even the wisest advice in this world would not have been useful at the time. That rigidity and the inability to have free choice did not match my cheerful and playful character.

We named our miracle child Ivan. He was different from his peers, and he showed it already in the first months of his life. His restless nature raised him to his feet at ten months, and at the age of one year he had already communicated with us. With that huge amount of energy he always carried with him as a knightly cloak, he was spreading joy and happiness everywhere he appeared. This unlimited euphoria was accompanied by countless questions and inexhaustible curiosity.

When he was three years old, he wanted to taste a beer. The next day he was playing, hitting himself in the head with a hammer and trying to understand its connection to pain. His curious and sometimes dangerous research had no end. Once he managed to climb up to the ceiling of the garage, and, delighted with the rotating fan, put his finger inside to see how it worked.

A similar incident happened when we were together on a bicycle. While he was sitting behind me, he put his foot on the wheel to see what would happen. He was a real "Dennis the Menace," who needed to know more about everything possible and impossible— at least to him. He had so much value and energy, but used his abilities against himself, even in his early childhood.

Today, I don't think he could have found his place in this world full of rules. His world was full of freedom and joy, and he showed us every day the mischief he could cause, knowing full well that everyone would still love him because his being was love, and he spread love wherever he went.

This reality constantly collided with his joyful and free world like two balloons that repel one another. And just when it would seem that lightness was approaching Ivan, the forces would turn into the opposite. What a challenge for a young mother, who had brought this beautiful being into this world, one with so much energy and joy, irresistible in his strangeness.

His curiosity did not only lead him in destructive directions. He learned quickly. He sang and played musical instruments. His intelligence had a constant need to seek and preserve new knowledge. His interests went from history, football, politics, and so on...constantly, quickly and briefly. He increased his knowledge on his own terms, in his own way.

He was a child born into a world that was not yet ready for him with boundless energy and joy, growing up with two parents fully occupied with their own egos, who put masks on their faces in the outside world and played the role of a perfect couple. Within the walls of our home the masks were removed. Anger and dissatisfaction, the endless struggle of two martyrs almost always leading to violent communication, took priority. Our separation actually started before the trappings of a home and furniture, but within that chaos, we managed to build a common life with unfinished bricks, and created something that on first sight looked like a family.

We moved to a new apartment where we initially slept on a carpet, but thoughts of filling it with furniture kept us thinking we would will fill the holes in our relationship. We believed that beautiful clothes, furniture, travel, would bring happiness. We missed the most important thing—harmony and joy.

The environment created a story about what my life should look like, and I agreed to it. I had that point of view that life is just like that.

I criticized my mother and father, but I created the same reality. I judged myself even more than them, and I was sure that everything was my fault. The only thing that gave me hope was belief that at some point something would happen that would prove that I was right. It would be revealed that everything is the way it should be. I just had to make an effort to be a good friend, a woman, a mother, and a colleague.

I lived in silent despair. It was a life of self-destruction. I had given so much importance to people and ties to others, instead of being free from everything and finding the joy within myself.

Read out.

Although it was a union I wanted, my husband and I created the same relationship as my parents—life in constant chaos. In the thirteen years of our marriage, the Creator, or what may be God in your world, has given us two children, Ivan, and later, my beautiful Alexandra.

Have we seen them as gifts? No, we did not, because we were too preoccupied with ourselves, with work, with our appearance in public, with other people.

Today, I would say that we slept through those years. Nobody was awake—not us, our friends, no one. Nothing was enough for us. It was only important what other people thought. We built our image like a tower of cards.

But who was I?

My body was trying to communicate with me in various ways, trying to warn me that something was wrong by creating a rash, fibromyalgia, an ulcer, and back pain. I suffered so much. And I did not pay attention to those messages.

How many judgments do you think I used to prove that I could succeed and be right? How much consciousness had I removed to be the image? When we "enter" into judging to prove something, we are removing our consciousness and our strength. That's exactly what I did.

☞ *See Coaching and Meditations, "The release of judgment," p. 124*

Today, when I use tools that contribute to people all over the world, every time I choose to think that I am right, I stop and ask myself a question:

"What is this? Do I want to be right or to be free?"

☞ *See Coaching and Meditations, "Full permission is the key to empowerment," p. 126*

Along with the changes inside of me, my outer world had changed, too. After years of fighting, divorce seemed to be the only solution that would give us a chance to focus our lives on another, perhaps a better direction for both of us. I moved into a friend's home for a while. I was not entirely ready for the next step. But I felt great happiness on the other side.

Now, there could be no mistakes. I knew everything was fine with me. I recognized the silent, but quite clear signals that my body sent about the new life that was evolving in me. I did not know whether to cry or to be happy.

Maybe it was a new beginning?

Believing in this, I gave another chance to the person who had destroyed, little by little, my illusions of eternal love.

The second miracle was born six years after Ivan on the 6th of August. Alexandra was completely different from her brother— calm, slow (or at least it looked like this after my experience with hyperactive Ivan), and not too demanding. A girl. A light that illuminated the world.

She was not more than ten when she wisely advised us:

"Mom and Dad, would you be so kind as to stop before you say something, and think about the situation, or to calmly talk?"

YOU ARE THE POWER

It was a completely different response to what the two of us would have considered on our own.

I remember once, while as an adult, she lived in Los Angeles and had a difficult exam coming up. She received an email from her friend with whom she was in disagreement at the time. When she did not open the message, at one point I asked:

"Aren't you interested in the message?"

She replied:

"Mom, if I open it now, it might upset me before the exam. I'll read it after the exam, because I do not want to deal with disagreements that are not a contribution for creating my life."

This is my daughter. And I'm very proud of her.

She is an incredible creator with a strong personality, despite all the experiences she had with us as a family. Quite the opposite of her brother, she chose a pragmatic way to observe the world around her.

There was not enough time or space in our lives for her while we lived together, even though she was not demanding. Our marriage was not better, but we persistently tried, as before, to fulfill what we missed in it, with the external values. We moved to a new house, decorated the home with as many beautiful things as possible, but with no warmth. We discovered new destinations that would at least create an illusion of us living the life we wanted. The days of days of joy and struggle, love and hate were replaced with things—no one had the courage or awareness to stop this program of our lives. We believed that we were doing the right thing and blind to any deep scanning of our emotions and real needs. Our children watched all this, and that formed their future.

☞ *See Coaching and Meditations, "Functioning from sorrow, pain and suffering," p. 127*

After twelve years, a wall finally appeared in front of us that we could not cross together.

My parents reacted furiously about my decision to move away.

"No matter how you feel, you do not leave the family and your husband." They were both incredibly together in their firmness this time. "You don't leave, you stay silent. That's how our ancestors lived. That's the way we live."

"NO! That was not to be my choice; I was clear and determined. At moments, it seemed like I was watching myself from the side and almost ready to applaud the woman who did not allow them to manipulate her anymore.

I was unwavering in my decision.

"What about the children?" everyone moaned.

I took the kids with me and started, I thought, a better life. But children do not have much understanding about adult fights. They just want their parents to be together. They want to continue to live in the world they are used to, a world that has its own frameworks, where they feel safe.

Ivan submitted to the divorce with difficulty, and he did everything in his power to draw our attention. We certainly did not behave like the best parents; we were preoccupied with our own egos, thinking that we are the ones who were most hurt. Even before the separation, Ivan was worried:

"Mom, who will build my dreams now and play Lego with me?"

I thought my love was enough. I was so convinced that I didn't even notice when he began to retreat into himself. The war that was happening between his father and me put him at the center of the storm.

Together we tried to console him in the moments of greatest sorrow he so openly showed. Without hiding anything, he constantly asked for answers, as he did in early childhood.

Alexandra was different. She took a step back and let us fight our own battle.

"Everything will be fine. We'll live with Dad for two weeks, and then two with Mom. You might like it. And they won't argue anymore," she tried to explain to her older brother.

Before long, I was a single mother trying to build a new life that would ultimately bring us all the peace and tranquility we desired. But the pain I carried about my husband and the failure of our dreams could not be reduced. He ruined all my carefully designed plans even when we were no longer together. In that condition, I was not aware of what was happening to my son. Later I found out that at the age of 13, he began to drink with his friends, trying to escape from his despair, and when that was not enough, he tried other things.

I was constantly looking for solutions that would help me. I was struggling with the feelings of pressure more and more, pulling out of me all the energy I was trying to gather for building a new world for myself and my children. I talked to doctors and psychologists, and they all gave me different answers, different programs. The only thing they offered was tranquilizers. It was a solution for me and for my son.

But was it really a cure for him? In fact, it invited him into the black market for something more, because those cures that were recommended for him did not manage to calm him down. On the contrary.

The consolation, which both of us needed, did not exist. I tried to find something other than medication, which did not have any positive effect on me. I discovered the twelve-step program of Alcoholics Anonymous, in which you are confronting yourself, saying that you are powerless against alcohol and you have no control.

Please, do not tell yourself that if you are in a similar situation! You are not powerless!

Of course, this doesn't mean that the program will not help you, but for me it was two years of confusion, especially the first step of accepting defeat and recognizing failure. The point of this first step was: "We confess that we are powerless against alcohol, that we cannot control our lives." The second step was: "We believe that a power greater than ourselves can bring back our mind."

It didn't work with me. I couldn't accept that I was powerless and that greater power than me could restore my common sense.

I can do it, just me, and no one else but me.

Today, I can observe that period of my life in a different, even compassionate, way, as someone who went through a script that they themselves would never write, not only for themselves, but for others as well.

At that time it was different. On the one hand, I was focused on my job. I was working in Sweden for a big American corporation as a project leader for bringing a new diversity philosophy to the company. I traveled all around the world to implement that philosophy in different countries. I worked hard to preserve the standard we had been building as a couple for years. I wanted my children to have everything and not to feel the absence of one parent. On the other hand, in struggling with my own feelings about someone who had been an equal participant in my life and who was now an enemy, I didn't notice what was most important—changes in my son.

Chapter *Four*

The first loss

It started with hashish and gravitated to heroin and cocaine. Ivan never got enough. He always needed something stronger that would bring him the bliss and joy that he so obsessively searched for, as if he could not breathe without it. He "ran" for that unreasonable joy during his entire childhood.

This life of his took place behind my back completely, which was the shadow of his true self—a gray, dark shadow. He was still emotional, gentle, kind. He showed unconditional love; nothing was defiled.

I loved him completely and infinitely. I was completely blind to the other, dark side of his life.

He was skilled at this. His behavior towards me and the words he sweetly spoke blurred my vision and perceptions. He would say to me:

"Mom, when you get older, you're going to live with me and my wife. I'll take care of you. You are the most beautiful mom in the world, in every way."

The first time he disappeared, it was for two days at the age of fifteen. For the next fifteen years, I tried to save him in all possible ways—from himself.

That led me to start wondering about the meaning of life. If there is a purpose, if happiness really exists, what is it? What is the feeling of waking up every morning and being happy for no reason? You know, happy, only happy!

Can you define happiness, touch it, and live it in the fullest sense? Is it a utopia, or are we just here for eating, sleeping, multiplying, and dying? Is that the meaning of life?

His first disappearance brought me an introduction, a first contact, with drugs. For those two interminable days, we did not have a trace, or hear a word from him, despite my desperate attempts to search every place I could remember in those totally mixed up and devastated moments. Every place? Some places did not even appear to me in the smallest parts of my mind.

"Who could have predicted this?" I asked myself and others. In my Universe, there was no awareness that something like this could happen.

Then, for the first time, I saw the other side of my angel. Just like the tattoo on his shoulder—on the right side was the devil, and on the left, Virgin Mary and the angel. His two main driving forces—one that was creative and one that was destructive. But what if it's just energy? Not good, not bad, but only a choice that creates the consciousness of your future? This was the thinking that would come to me, later.

After this first incident, when I found him almost unconscious, we talked for hours, and, of course, I again believed his words because they sounded so honest. How can you not trust a child when he says with the purest of emotions:

"Mom, I will never do it again. Never! I promise!"

Well, that would have been a happy story... *Everyone can make a mistake*. But, it was not. It got worse. And nothing helped.

I threatened, shouted, begged, tried to understand, and it was not worth it. The more I tried to get him out of his demonic embrace, the worse it got—guilt, regret, anger, sorrow, shame—all these feelings and emotions completely dominated our lives, like a barrage of boats on a turbulent sea.

"There is no justice in this world," I thought. "He was an angel, a special being. Why did he choose this way?"

I remember one year during the holidays I sent him to the village with his grandmother, to Serbia. He liked to hang out with children. It did not matter whether someone was poor, messy, or dirty. He would bring them home to feed them if they were hungry. His generosity was limitless. He shared meals or money with those who needed it and never understood why there were separations between people.

"I do not understand why people act like that. Well, if those who have too much would share with those who do not have, everything would be settled," he said.

He was full of love that he unselfishly expressed through hugs, kisses, and tenderness. He immediately wanted and tried to solve any vague communication or disagreement between us, because he could not live in silence and anger.

He was a child with symptoms we today call "sensitive child," "OCD," (obsessive-compulsive disorder) and "ADHD" (hyperactivity). Everything about him was too exaggerated, too pronounced, too vigorous.

Even I judged him in a different way. I did not see him in the right light, as he really was. I tried to soothe him in the same way my parents had with me, but I did not have the tools or the understanding then.

Despite all the promises, a few months later, the darkness returned.

One morning, which gave no hint of the pain to come, I went into his room and found him shivering in bed, as if sprinkled with freezing rain from above. He was completely pale, and with his eyes blown up in fear, he pointed to the window and spoke so quietly that I could hardly understand:

"Look at them," he said. "They will enter the room. See how big they are!"

"What are you talking about?" I tried to understand, looking through the glass where I saw nothing but the outline of trees and roofs.

"They're huge," he continued. "Snakes! How can you not see?!" He was persistent.

I hugged him and tried to calm him down, but his irrational fear was not something my rational mind could understand. That was the moment that started my search for answers, to save my son, a struggle for which, at times, I was ready to give up my own life.

Joy completely disappeared from our reality.

At seventeen, he decided to live with a girlfriend, and from that moment on his everyday life for me became hazy, but I could tell things weren't right. He never had a job, he slept until noon, and played video games with friends. On the other hand, his exceptional intelligence and volcanic energy pushed him towards new passions and interests. Unfortunately, this never turned into anything serious because of his lack of concentration. The occasional "drug trip" became part of our reality, but I never knew how long it would last and how hard it would be to get through. Chaotic thoughts rushed through my head, incapable of turning into any common sense.

The first visit to the hospital was terrible, because it was against his will.

His girlfriend called me at four o'clock in the morning. She said that Ivan was walking up and down the stairs in their building with a knife in his hand, because he thought he was being chased by the police.

We left him at the hospital for a month and he was angry.

"I hate you," my angel said to me.

The words crushed my heart, my love, my life, but I was persistent. I could not give up. What could I do? My only choice was to help my son.

After the anger passed, well into a month of treatment, he became even more sensitive.

He stayed with me for several weeks after that first incident. By the look in his eyes and the way he spoke, as if floating amongst the clouds, and by uncontrolled laughter that spread like a fire around the room, I realized that he was taking drugs again. His eyes were staring at me like huge balls, but without light, just a dark cavity you could easily fall into forever. It seemed that all the sadness of this world was reflected in them. Ivan never cried. He just looked so lost.

He did not understand my anger, only his own.

When the drugs took over his life, sensitivity, care and tenderness still existed, but also immense sorrow. Just looking at him, my heart cracked into tiny pieces. I felt as though I was treading on glass on the floor with my own weight. He could have been without food for days, but he did not ask for help. Except once.

He came to me completely exhausted, so thin, almost transparent, and with all that sadness he had carried in and around himself, said:

"Help me detoxify my body."

We live in a reality in which many people look at the use of drugs as a nice experience. But everyone forgets that it can only be so in the beginning and that this feeling will not last. The true space of peace, joy, bliss and ecstasy is not available, palpable, when we are under the influence of drugs. It's only a suppression of our true state, not a means to it. It will take you away from your life.

☞ *See Coaching and Meditations, "Why do you refuse to receive consciousness?," p. 128*

From his fifteenth to the thirtieth year, Ivan's life had only one goal—rescue from drugs. During this period, he lived for almost ten years with his girlfriend. He said that she was the only one who understood him, although they were completely different. She had a permanent job; she took care of the house. At first glance it would seem that he lived a normal life. I was grateful for every day that flowed without problems and drama. When he lived alone, every visit to him broke my heart, because I would find him without food, since he spent all his money on drugs.

My mother adored and protected him. Just like me, after all.

"Let him take drugs, it's only important that he is alive," she'd say.

Although it was hard for her to show her feelings and tenderness, there was nothing she wouldn't do for Ivan. She bought him the most expensive wardrobe, paid his bills, and cleaned his apartment.

"He is the light of my life," she'd explain.

After his death, a part of her died with him. I believe that she left her body at the same time Ivan left our earthly life. Emotionally, they were buried together.

Ivan was so cute and manipulated us easily. But he never understood what he was doing.

If I asked him why he had taken drugs, he'd answer:

"Mom, why are we always having the same conversation? Why can't you live your life and let me live mine?"

After that, he'd add:

"Mom, do you realize how much I love you and how grateful I am? You're all I have!"

His father could not deal with his son's pain, so he chose to escape. I tried to include him in our agony, called him to help me, but he chose his way. And nothing is wrong with that. We all deal differently with the feelings that crush our gut with an iron fist. His way was to stir up a stone wall of anger where reality could not penetrate, unless on his terms.

"Call me when he gets rid of drugs, then we can talk," he'd say to me when I asked for help with our son.

One week before he left our lives, Ivan came to me:

"Mom, I want to go see Dad, I want to talk to him and tell him that I am angry too, but we need to calm down and reconcile," he said convincingly.

He did what he said, but his father refused to give him the help he asked for. He called me after leaving his father's house, disappointed:

"Mom, this is the last time I will see him. I will not ask for his love anymore. I'm free. Maybe you do not believe me, but I'm free. It's over! I'm done with him. I want to put an end to our relationship and start taking care of my life and start all over again. I'm done with drugs. I want to start a new life." His conviction was palpable.

It wasn't the first time I'd heard him say that. I'd been listening to such promises ever since I realized that he was taking drugs. Ivan was in detox 18 times over 15 years, and every time he said he would stop drugs. What I didn't know at that time was that after seeing his father, he went from the airport directly to the hospital and checked himself into a drug withdrawal treatment. But only two days after that he left the hospital.

I didn't see him after that; we just exchanged phone messages that would play out like this:

"Ivan, I will not come to the hospital to visit you. No! That's my choice. If you don't want to live, there's nothing more I can do."

I was not giving up on him. I was just sick and tired of doing the same thing all over again. So, I choose to be in allowance of his choices. I was pulling out of a drama that no longer served us. His pattern of being hospitalized for a week to get off drugs, then out on the streets again and with the same friends, living the same life—I was not willing to support that game anymore. I was done.

"Mom, believe me! This is the last time you will have to come to the hospital. Everything has changed, and I promise that I will always be there for you."

These are the last words I heard. It was Monday. He was killed on Friday.

Beginning of summer. Midsummer...

I usually did not go this long without hearing from him. But is this really important? We are never separated! Not then, not even when he was killed, not even now. Never! He is just no longer in physical form. He is here even now, he writes with me, and he listens, inspires, enjoys. He laughs loudly, takes up space with his endless energy, which, if it can be described in simple words—is everywhere, and in everything.

The drugs opened the door to hell for him in many ways, including increasing his innate sensitivity and his reactions to certain circumstances. They took all his life's joy. He was no longer a participant in his life; he chose to erase the present. In his world, this wasn't important any more. The drugs took control of him, chose everything instead of him, created for him, and he disappeared, no longer existed, as though a transparent shield of the former person. Even before he went out of our lives.

☞ *See Coaching and Meditations, "Living from joy," p. 128*

I'd lost him a long time ago, but I just couldn't accept it. I did not want to. He was trapped in his feelings, emotions and tormented thoughts, and he always found reasons and excuses why he could not change his life.

He used to say:

"Hashish is not dangerous." Or, "You have friends who do the same thing, you just do not know."

He shared his pain, his problems, his despair with people who had similar experiences, similar feelings. We judged him for drug abuse, and he condemned himself because he disappointed us.

This circle of punishment, rewards and judgments, is never complete. It lasts in an infinite loop: from defense, justification, resistance, reaction, and to the present in which he no longer exists.

All these years I have lived on a constant seesaw. When we broke up, my husband left me the mortgage on our house and other financial dealings. At one point, he even disappeared, fleeing from any responsibility.

I started asking the Universe:

- What else is possible?

- Where can I learn something different, and who can help me?

This cannot be real!

There must be something else!

I was angry, as anyone would be in that situation.

My health began to collapse. I had eczema all over my body, everything hurt—my back, my head, my bones...

Everyone said it was hereditary because my mom had rheumatism. But I did not agree with that. I read, swallowing everything I could find about the connection between the physical and emotional states. A different truth opened up to me. I discovered new views, new possibilities that showed me that there might be "something else," that this narrow space in which we exist is not the only thing available to us.

Where am I? Where am I going?

I kept working overtime, studied, cared for sick parents, all while enduring an ongoing, silent war with my ex-husband. Ivan went his own way.

At one point, I could no longer continue. I was seriously ill.

One morning at work, I felt I was losing myself. I sat like a statue, and no longer "had" a right hand. The feeling was just like that. I saw my arm, but I did not feel it. I was disappearing.

The doctors thought I was paralyzed. I cannot remember anything further from that day. But when I woke up the next day, I could walk. And what do you think I did?

I went straight to work.

However, my body rebelled and tied me to bed for the next six weeks.

I was angry at the Universe; at everything.

I clearly remember the moment when I said to myself: "Wait! I'm stronger than all this."

I returned home, cried for two days like a little child, screaming because of the pain, and through meditation and yoga, wondered: "What else is possible for me?"

I was looking for something still intangible in my mind that could get me out. I knew it existed on some level.

☞ *See Coaching and Meditations, "What do we create?," p. 129*

The next step was to resign from the company I had worked at for almost 20 years. I felt the CEO was disappointed because he had a vision of me one day becoming HR Manager and maybe moving to Chicago, so in his eyes I had failed. But the burden of working in a challenging role with conflicting philosophies— bringing American leadership to our country—was too much for me at that time. It was as though, at one point, life swept down like a huge crane and collapsed me, pressing me down. I couldn't breathe. I *forgot* to breathe. I knew that I couldn't endure this feeling too long without obvious consequences. It seemed I had no way out. But then, I found a way.

In the northern part of Sweden, there is an island where an unusual art therapy called Vedic Art is practiced. Vedic Art is an intuitive painting method, that allows you to connect with your heart and let your inner world manifest on an empty canvas. The 17 principles come from the ancient Indian teachings, the Vedas, which is said to be the knowledge we have within us. It is said that all the energies of the world are being accumulated there, on a land were powerful Vikings once passed.

I packed up, even though I could hardly walk, and went there to isolate. I started to paint. I had a small sleeping area where I could hug myself in sleep, in a huge covered cabin, which reminded me of a barn in my village, where the locals kept the cows. In contrast to the sleeping area, the rest of the space was large, illuminated by the incredible light that came in from all sides, like a multitude of magical suns.

Everyone there had their own space for healing, and a part of the wall on which to create, to express. Each of us got our share of light, peace and quiet, in which, in some moments, seemed endless. I painted the wall from one side to the other, sometimes with strong strokes, sometimes with gentle strokes, the colors in some moments streaming out like joy, sometimes like sorrow. Everything I was feeling I transferred to the wall. I cried, then painted, and then cried again.

I prayed, pulled power in, and filled myself with it. And I cured myself. Alone. Or, not alone?

It wasn't until two years later that I came upon the teachings of Gary Douglas and Dr. Dain Heer, founders of Access Consciousness, which would later prove to have an enormous impact on the trajectory of my life.

Chapter *Five*

When murder invades

Anger is an acid that can do more harm to the vessel in which it is stored than to anything on which it is poured.

—MARK TWAIN

When I opened my eyes that morning, June 24, 2010, I felt heaviness in the air. My body would not accept a change in position and wanted to stay in its comfortable, lying state. At first, I thought to cancel my departure for the celebration and spend the day in complete lethargy, with the desire to stop time for a moment. Where did this feeling come from? But I decided to venture into the happy world that was preparing for the coming of the warmest season, where spring and summer energies are combined and together create magical sparks of new possibilities.

In Sweden, the Solstice (Midsummer), celebrating the longest day of the year, is one of the grandest and happiest holidays. After this day, the sun begins its retreat earlier, allowing the darkness in sooner and longer.

In a country where the summer is only a random passerby, who doesn't stay very long, it's natural to celebrate the arrival of light and warmth with added exuberance. The days around Midsummer feel as though there is no sunset, and light triumphs in every way. A few days before the celebration, everyone is preparing; euphoria begins to spread from one house to another like a wave, and the streets are filled with joy that cradles the silver birches and their shimmering blooms.

Many of the people start the holiday with the traditional picking of flowers for making wreaths—beautiful crowns woven from nature, worn in untamed hair with special joy. The beauty of the light shines from all sides, from inside and out. People eat fresh fish, and drink cold beer and plenty of domestic brandy. And they play and dance in complete elation on a green carpet where nature can finally be revealed in its entire splendor, while the sound of a far off orchestra reverberates off a stone hill from the opposite shore.

For most Swedes, but also for many foreigners who are in the country at the time and fortunate to attend a celebration, it is simply the best party of the year.

On one such wonderful and cheerful night—murder invaded and turned my life upside down. It came without a call, without warning, without any sense— *Is there any sense to murder ever?*

Something happened. Something that was not supposed to happen. Something that has never, even been in the most hidden tunnels of our consciousness.

That year, the celebration began with noise and joy, as always. I was surrounded by close friends I had known for more than fifteen years. We laughed and took pictures, decked out in crowns of flowers. We danced and sang the traditional "Små grodona," which translates to English as "Little frogs," ate herrings and potatoes and juicy strawberries for dessert that melted on our palates.

Everything felt like magic pouring down from heavenly heights, but I did not feel calm. It was as though totally opposite emotions had mixed into a glowing ball that pulsed in my stomach. Though there was incredible energy and joy, there was also a sense of discomfort. Everyone told me they had never seen me so bright and happy. I felt free from everything, but still...

A few weeks before that, I had attended an Access Consciousness course, where I accessed all of me! This feeling of excitement— butterflies in your stomach like you are in love, no limitations, you love everything and you are totally connected to everything— managed to transcend my body, making it feel infinitely expansive and happy. When I arrived home, people asked if I was in LOVE! And I said YES! With me! A presence of being, knowing that the space I had within me was all that I needed and all that I am. This is where the healing began. I accessed JOY and the potency of being me! My body was in rhythm with the wave of a higher level of energy where molecules are in connection with everything, revealing possibilities, joy, ease, and the art of receiving.

I had just moved into a new apartment and was ready to embrace a new phase, free from everything that had ruined my life and my health in the previous years.

For the first time in my life, I lived alone. Until then, the children would occasionally come and go, continuing a circle of warmth.

But now, in this smaller apartment, I only had room for me. It was time for my children to become responsible and live their lives.

Around eight o'clock that evening, a strange feeling of restlessness overtook me. Although my friends persuaded me to stay with them, because the party was at its peak, something told me that I should leave. Cold space, as if I had entered a large freezer, surrounded my body, sending signals that I did not recognize and that were not pleasant to me. I felt pressure in my chest, as if iron clamps were tightening me. I could not even recognize what this feeling might be. I felt like I was receiving something, messages that I could not decrypt. But where did these messages come from? How?

During the celebration, I was constantly trying to call my son to see if everything was okay, even though I knew he would be angry and tell me as always: *Mom, I'm thirty, stop treating me like I'm a child.*

But something, something sent signals to me that day. *Consciousness? Maternal instinct? Energy?*

Two hours later I finally managed to leave the party as things were winding down. A thin thread of festivity remained with me when I got home, and so I posted a few photos from the celebration on Facebook, sharing moments of a country's common joy with my friends.

The sound of the phone upset my quiet contemplation. It was already midnight, and I thought it was a mistake, because I did not recognize the number. I was surprised by a woman's voice who asked without introducing herself:

"Did you see on the news about your son?"

It is impossible to describe that moment. It's almost impossible to get it back from this deep gap in the past. The moment when everything stopped, and I heard myself, as if I were in the distance, ask:

"What are you talking about?"

"I saw it on the news! I saw it on the news!," the voice in the handset exclaimed.

Even today I don't know who that woman was. Everything after that conversation took over my life, and I did not have the strength to go back and discover who this person was, which in the first moments didn't even reach my mind.

I turned on the TV and heard myself talking to her, hoping that she would tell me it was some kind of joke:

"I do not see anything. It sounds so bizarre. I'll call the police."

And I called. I introduced myself, assuming their answer would be, *Who's joking with you?*

But I heard something completely different:

"We'll be with you in ten minutes."

It seemed as though they had flown the distance between the police station and my apartment, as though they were in front of the door of my new home in a moment. Without looking directly at me, they entered the kitchen, turned from one side to the other, as if they themselves did not know what to do. They asked me if I had a friend who could come immediately. I did not understand. Why are they insisting for someone to be with me, why don't they tell me anything? In my head I held the idea that a fight had happened, and Ivan was in jail.

Everything that followed was wrapped in a thick, opaque fog, which turned a beautiful summer day into the coldness night of my life.

In that kitchen, something else took control, as if you could touch the energy that settled in my Universe as the police entered the room. It's a moment when we freeze and when everything stops, when we realize there is nothing more that can help us avoid the pain. When we are filled with so much dense energy that it's as if our heads are packed in armor so that we do not hear anything, we do not see, we do not feel. There is no world around us, only complete emptiness. It is not easy to describe this destruction, when the only thing you feel is that your heart will explode. And disappear.

It seems quite absurd that at a moment like this, my awareness was greater than I could ever think possible—the concern that my daughter Alexandra would find out about her brother's death before she heard it from me was almost as big as the sorrow of knowing my son was dead.

At that time she lived in Los Angeles, and news from Sweden might have missed her, if not for social media. I asked a friend of ours who lived in LA to call her and keep her talking because the news was already on Facebook. Our friend jumped in the car and kept Alexandra on the phone all the way from Santa Monica to Hollywood. When she entered her apartment, she called me and gave the phone to Alex so I could tell her. She cried, I heard her screams through the phone, and I felt every part of her pain, although she was thousands of miles away. Or was she?

I felt as though we were ONE, and the distance was completely gone. I could feel every breath, every emotional blink of her being, and I knew that I had to take a completely different attitude, first of all because of her, so that she could bear all the horror that had come to our life. At that moment, my choice was to stay calm.

The first month after the murder, everything was wrapped in a mist shrouding the pain and preventing its lifting. When the investigation was completed, my family and I saw the body for the first time. But, there was nothing in his body anymore. There was only the membrane, the frame of his former being. It was merely the wrapper that covered my Ivan.

My mother and father were screaming in pain, and I stood to the side like a stone. I could not get any closer, because there was a body that I did not recognize any more. I scanned it, and when I got to his feet, I only looked at him once. At that moment I felt peace. He is now quiet. And I went outside.

During that cold afternoon, which seemed to belong to someone else rather than me, Gary Douglas, the founder of Access Consciousness, called all of the facilitators across the globe to contribute to the energy of peace. He did not know that I would be standing next to a dead son.

But did this information reach my mind then?

Perhaps much, much later.

The funeral was beautiful. More than a hundred people, from all sides, came to be with us that day. The environment was of young men and women who wore grief in their hearts, but their outward appearance was in absolute contrast.

My daughter and I asked everyone to come dressed in white.

We knew that this was not a definite departure; it was Ivan's next step on his journey. He was not dead for us. There was a body, or a frame of his body, in this life, but HE went back to ONENESS, where we all belong. He stepped towards something better and bigger.

We witnessed one completely unacceptable moment in our reality, something that should not have happened. I was standing there, burying my son. It should not have been that way. I should have died before him. I whispered to a friend who was standing next to me that I could not stand it, that I could not deal with what I felt. But at the same time, I realized I must be strong because of my daughter.

I turned into a rock on whose face sorrow could not appear.

Ivan was in my new apartment only once, and he did not like it. He commented:

"Oh, Mom, you moved so far. I want to be near you."

Now he is close; the cemetery is not far.

How is it possible that my son was killed on the day of the greatest celebration? What reason can be so important? Why do we choose it? What is the punishment, and how to deal with it? *Why?*

Are these the right questions? No. We will never find the answers. The reason for Ivan's murder? The conclusion at the trial was: unknown. It was cold-blooded murder, for no reason. And they did not just kill him, they massacred him. *Why?* And who were they at that moment? Were they people, animals, addicts, demons? Or were they just ordinary people with too many drugs in their physical bodies suppressing all molecules of consciousness?

One of the demons who killed my son got 18 months in jail and the other one, life, which, in Sweden is a maximum of 18 years.

Here is one possible story about what happened that summer night, which I learned after the trial, when I could hear it.

Two young men, who did not know each other, met on a bus. One of them had just gotten out of jail, and the other was a drug addict from Stockholm, who came to our city for a new life. They were bored. They started to talk and discovered that they had a common acquaintance. A friendship was created and, so they decided to leave the bus together for a beer. They tried to reach their common friend, but he didn't answer the phone. So, they started to consider his whereabouts.

In the meantime, they added hashish, cocaine, and some pills to the beer. In their twilight state of mind, an *image* was created—that another shared acquaintance, Ivan—may have been responsible for the disappearance of their friend. The *vision* was upgraded to a crime scenario in which their acquaintance was being held by the mafia in Ivan's apartment, so they had to get him out. Equipped with a hammer, scissors, knives and other weapons, which they hid in the pockets of their jackets, they went to my son's apartment.

Ivan didn't suspect anything; he was home with a friend talking about girls. The day stretched out with summer rest, and when the visitors rang, Ivan did not want to open the door at first. Was there a trace of doubt in his head, or was it just a desire not to interrupt the moment of conversation?

"What do you want?" he asked.

"We have something for you," they replied.

Two young men entered the apartment with a bag.

Ivan asked curiously:

"What do you have for me?"

"Look in the bag," said the one who had just gotten out of jail.

According to the friend who was with Ivan at that time, that is when the bloody "feast" began.

When Ivan bent down to look at the bag, he was hit over the head with a hammer. He fell down immediately. We don't know exactly what happened after that, but in a state of the most unimaginable chaos and turmoil, the frenzied barefoot boy ran out to the street, concealing himself in dark corners from the anger of the killers who followed him. For the next few hours, he was not able to move because of the fear, keeping himself in the darkness—the best shelter. But they found him. The darkened minds created a massacre. My son had more than one hundred stings on his body.

What dark forces propelled two young men to commit such a crime? They had no moral comprehension of what they had done. Afterwards, they behaved as if they had stolen a chocolate in the shop. They told a few people that they might have done *something*, clumsily trying to hide the traces. The police found them easily that same evening.

Why did they do it?

I still haven't read the police report. It's too painful to see the details of what they did to my son. It sits locked in a box in the basement, in the darkness where it belongs. My son wasn't just killed; he was abused, tortured, massacred.

Why?

Why?

Why?

The answer has yet to arrive—from the two monsters who performed this brutal act, from the police, from anyone. Why couldn't they just give us the answer and release us from the circle of doubt, wonder, uncertainty, pictures made up in our minds of how it all went down?

Is there an answer at all?

What does an answer even mean in this reality where he no longer exists?

There were two of them. I do not understand how it could be possible that neither of them thought to stop, at any moment. Just stop and let my boy live.

If we really become conscious beings, would we kill each other?

Would we destroy each other?

Who will take responsibility for what happened—the murderers, society, family, God, Ivan or simply—no one?

How are we going to live now? What is life? Why do we live?

These questions shifted around in my mind during the trial in December.

Discovering the answers is my path today and will be until I find them, no matter where and when. These are the questions I seek answers to; not the others.

I cried when nobody watched and screamed when no one listened.

And I did something because I just wanted to get away from these devastating feelings, but people began to judge me.

What choices do you have when your child dies? You can die, too, or you can survive.

I took all the money I had and fled to Costa Rica, to a resort where people are isolated from the outside world.

ı remember the moment I arrived in this paradise on Earth. The sadness and anger in me were mixed with a beautiful environment that seemed to coddle me.

Nature was vibrating all around us. I felt its full beauty while we worked on the Energy Synthesis of Living program through Access Consciousness with Dr. Dain Heer and Gary Douglas. It was easy to join in synthesis with plants and nature, in this magical earthly garden. I felt that the plants gave me energy and strength, and that my cells vibrated. It was one completely indescribable experience of being.

We lived in complete harmony with nature, as part of it, and in some moments, we merged with it—with these incredible scents, with the song of birds we had never seen before, with the whispering of rainforests, with an endless green carpet that stretched to infinity...I had never before experienced this symbiosis between our bodies and our environment.

"Can I die here?" I asked Gary.

After each training, my life showed up to give me a hand; my joy briefly returned to signal that it was coming back to me. And I decided to continue, to move on, and to give that feeling a chance to lead me. For the next year, I followed Gary and Dain all over the world. I learned, healed myself, and returned to life. They gave me incredible support, and I am grateful to them forever.

But people judged me. My friends. My parents. They said: "How can you go to Costa Rica?", "How can you post photos of you laughing when your son is dead?", "Why are you celebrating your birthday when your son is dead?"

Did they really know how I felt?

Did they ever ask me?

NO!

Nobody knew how angry I was—angry at Ivan. And hurt. I could only tell that to him, at the place where his body was sleeping, the body he chose in this reality.

He said that he would always be there for me, always, as I was for him.

Why didn't he keep his promise?

I was angry at the killers, too, and energetically demanded their apology, to stop the suffering they caused me. Honestly, I prayed that they felt much more suffering than was mine, for all time. When I went to the grave, I prayed that my son's murderers get all this in return, and I prayed that someone kill them even worse than they had destroyed Ivan.

What are they? And what does the drug do to a human being when it becomes a beast to massacre another human being like that?

Where do the demons come in? What did they actually see? Certainly, they didn't see a man, Ivan.

That's how it was then! But that has changed.

Can I forgive now?

Yes. I can say that. I want them to get consciousness. This is my greatest wish for them, to find light.

Since then, the day of greatest joy each year becomes the day of greatest sadness for me, and I spend it mostly by myself, meditating and connecting with my son.

After Ivan's death, several of his close friends stopped using drugs. My son didn't know what to do with his life, and perhaps his life was the contribution to other people to find their own meaning.

The right way to "deal"

What is the right way to deal with a situation like this? If this hadn't happened to me, I'd have plenty of answers. Now I know that in times when something directly affects us, there is no right or wrong answer or action. The best thing we can do at those moments is to allow our environment to give us choices, not to judge us, and not to expect us to behave a certain way, regardless of whether it takes a year or a decade.

Judgments from my friends and family and their projections of how I should behave were more for themselves, than being supportive of me and my daughter during this period.

Why do we like to judge other people?

Who are we to do it?

Is there something that we have not been, or did not do in life?

My choice was to consider that this was coming from them, where they function from, and to be in allowance of their judgments of me.

Their reactions were based on their own judgments and convictions necessary to deal with their own situations, or their own projections onto my situation, based on the experiences and limitations they chose in their own lives at certain times. And nothing is either good or bad in that. It's just a choice.

The fact that I chose something different at that moment did not seem like a conscious choice, it's just a choice that brought me to where I am today in my life.

Or maybe it was a conscious choice?

And is death the end?

No it's not! It cannot be! Death can never be the end. Death is the path, and life is a traveler. Soul is a guide. When a traveler is tired and exhausted, the guide gives instructions for short or long rests, and then the journey begins again.

Our mind thinks of death. Our heart thinks of life.

And its light above us.

And, what did I choose?

I chose to be alive and live in full capacity.

I chose joy and gratitude.

I chose to take risks and never give up.

I chose to ask questions.

I invite you to continue in the next pages of this book to learn more about these choices—why I made them, how I managed to find my way, and how you may choose them, or your own, for the journey you are on. I will also offer coaching and meditations that can help anyone find their own life's meaning.

Do you live your life?

Or did your environment create your life?

What choices have you made?

What choices could you make?

PART III
Different Choices

CHOOSING TO BE ALIVE AND LIVE FULLY

CHOOSING JOY AND GRATITUDE

CHOOSING TO TAKE RISKS AND NEVER GIVE UP

CHOOSING TO ASK QUESTIONS

If you had only ten seconds left for the rest of your life, what would you choose?

Everything is choice. Everything is infinite possibility. Everything is the question, nothing is the answer. Be you and change the world, be not you and suffer the world. Truth is your sword, choice is your creation. Being is the destruction of all limitation to be you. You are the gift. As you be the gift, you shall receive. So as you be, you shall receive, different reality. Be it, claim, own, decide, create it. Live not in the effect of life, but as the source of it. Know you as the greatness, perceive you as the greatness, be you as the greatness, and receive you as the greatness, because that is the truth.

—GARY DOUGLAS, FOUNDER, ACCESS CONSCIOUSSNESS

What else is possible?

All of us who look for access to awareness, know we already have it, we WERE consciousness, but we may have forgotten, and we just need to be reminded. I want to bring you back to that memory with this next section of this book about choices. You know who you are, you have access to consciousness; you just forgot how to use it.

Through this book you will get tools to remind you where you are from. We are here because of experiences. And because we know why we are here, we should not give so much importance to it, but to "be in allowance and gratitude." I am grateful for 30 years of life with my son, for the experiences I had with him, which we created together, and now I am grateful for every moment I spend with my daughter, for her words, even when we quarrel, because that's what we both want to have as our experience. We are never alone, and we can never create the same moment in life.

So, how would it be for us to accept ourselves in total light and with joy? And when we say something, let's realize that this is not eternal and that we do not lock ourselves in pain, suffering and judgment. Because this judgment separates us from one another and makes it true. And it's not. These are lies from our old beliefs that we drag through time and we cannot get rid of them because we forgot to access consciousness.

Remember who you are!

Your imperfections, your defects, your uniqueness are what make you so real and brilliant, so great, crazy, beautiful, human. Even in your imperfection, you are always the perfect expression of life, the beloved child of the Universe, a complete work of art, unique in the whole world, and you deserve all the wealth of life. It's not a matter of being just perfect as "you." It's always about being present, being here, choosing and experiencing the magic of your life. "There is a crack in everything, that's how the light gets in," sings Leonard Cohen.

After the death of my son, I became aware of what exactly is—my energy. It's a gift. And you have it, we all have it. Most people do not realize that they are a gift to the world and that their body is a gift and a miracle. People do the opposite—they judge themselves and do not think of themselves as something very important to this world. If you are kind, caring, joyful, and human—you are a gift! If you focus on opportunities, not on the obstacles, and if you feel that this world can be a better place, you are a gift! If you look at others without a point of view and without judging, you are a gift!

What can you "bring" to this world? What contribution can you be to the lives of other people? How to be an inspiration to each other— TODAY?

When my vibration changed, the external situation changed, as if the magic interfered. Yes, magic.

Chapter *Six*

Choosing to be alive and live fully

What is death after all? Death is a sleeping child.
And what is life? Life is a child that is playing,
singing and dancing at every moment before
the Father. Death is the sleeping child inside the
Heart of the Inner Pilot. Life is inspiration. Life
is aspiration. Life is realisation. Life is not the
reasoning mind. Life is not the intellectual mind.
Life is not a game of frustration. No, life is the
message of divinity on Earth.

—SRI CHINMOY

Two weeks after my son's death, in complete despair, I sent an email to my friend Dr. Dain Heer:

"I will no longer deal with Access. I give up." I was sobbing, failing to catch my breath.

Even in a dream, I did not expect the following sentence, but it came from him straight and clear:

"You can kill yourself and become the real effect of your son's death, or you can start to live."

At that moment, its sense could not reach me. My first reaction was:

"This man is not normal! What is he talking about?!"

Anger wrapped me as a heavy blanket.

"He does not care about me!"

But later, this incredible sentence found its way to my consciousness, and I realized that he didn't allow me to get into the role of the victim, but gave me the energy to stand in my capacity.

What do we need to reach that capacity?

How many of us are walking down the street, and in fact we're dead?

And what do we need to feel alive? To choose life?

What would you choose?

Will you continue to use that pathetic energy against yourself?

I can tell you that you are the person who can change the whole world. Will you finally "get into" that capacity? How would it look like to see what you have, rather than constantly complaining? To be grateful, as Gary Douglas told me.

At that time, my life was covered with sorrow that connected my parents, my daughter, friends and all the people who felt pain because of the loss of this wonderful boy, Ivan.

Did we really lose him? Or are we so programmed to believe that we lose somebody when death comes?

Honestly, if I had to go back at that time and describe the moments that followed Ivan's death, that would be impossible, because my memory was wrapped in an opaque membrane. In order to survive, I just excluded my true self from my being and focused on practical funeral matters. It was an easier way than dealing with my emotions. They were waiting.

All the tools that I have ever learned were a great help. I received support from all sides: from the Universe, from the environment, mostly from my daughter, though I wasn't aware of it at the time. Today, I am immensely grateful for that.

I kept asking the same question: If absolutely everything is our choice, why did Ivan choose to be killed?

According to the philosophy of the ancient Indian scriptures about the essence of life (the Upanishads), death is nothing but a change of body. At some point, the soul decides to discard it as we toss our dirty clothes aside in the evening. Human life is the period when we clean and improve ourselves in order to reach the ultimate bliss. This process takes place through a multitude of births.

We've all lived countless lives before this moment, and we meet again in order to live new experiences. There is nothing we haven't been, or done. We were all murderers, we've all been killed. We were kings and beggars. What if the Universe or God evolves through us?

One of my favorite spiritual leaders is Sri Chinmoy. In his book *Death and Reincarnation*, he wrote:

"Life begins with the form of minerals, and we are heading to plant formations. Then we enter the kingdom of animals. From that place we come to the world of human beings. But that's not the end. Our goal is to become divine beings."

What if Ivan sacrificed himself in order to create a higher awareness?

His death shook the entire city. In the world of his friends, nothing was the same. Their lives were radically changed.

So, his death has contributed to human consciousness. What a fantastic contribution!

Believe it—death does not exist! The occasion we call death only helps us to rest and change. And to return with new hopes and new life. When a loved one goes, do not worry. Cry, scream, yes— why not? And respect your memories, but do not worry. That's what I did. I went to the cemetery every morning and cried, and I was arguing with him, because I was very, very angry. I said to him:

"How could you do this to me? You promised that you would always be with me, that one day when I got old, you would take care of me."

But, in fact, he didn't go anywhere, he did not leave me. He is right there! And he does take care of me. He has shown me his presence in many ways and in different forms. He sent messengers with messages that only I could understand. Many people came to tell me that he appeared in their dreams and explained to them how to find me.

One day, an unknown girl from another city knocked at my door. Although she was so confused, she resolved to convey this message:

"A young man came to me in a dream and told me where to find you, to tell you that it was his choice and not to be unhappy about it," she said clearly.

He was with me all the time, and he showed himself through other people, reminding me that he was here, that he didn't go anywhere, he didn't disappear. I have never met so many people named Ivan in my life, even when I least expected it. His name kept appearing in unlikely places along my daily path.

At that time, I had already been conducting workshops in Croatia and Serbia, where I transfer the knowledge I have been studying for years, not only through Access Consciousness, but through other techniques. As if everything I learned was waiting to come out of me and start the transformations of other people, in addition to my own.

I started to wonder: Where is my power required? Where is my energy sought? How can I contribute? What contribution can I be on planet Earth, and how can I transform all this knowledge into education?

It was time for me to give something back to this reality.

My journey led to Zagreb, and then to Belgrade. Ivan was with me—my unexpected support.

I was holding a workshop located on the first floor, and when I first got there, I saw that the name Ivan was written in capital letters, on the door in front of me. Each morning, this inscription welcomed me, and I saw it upon my departure every evening. He was there in the beginning of every day, and at its end.

His name has followed me wherever I go.

From Belgrade, I went to Opatija and arrived at accommodations near the church of St. Ivan. For me, these were special signs that made me stronger, because I felt that he was with me all the time. The next day, at the workshop, it was surprising to me that the son of my organizer was also called Ivan.

People at the workshops spoke about feeling his presence and precisely described him, though they'd never met.

One day, while I was at a camp in Costa Rica, an unknown woman came and sat beside me. At first I was confused, but I quickly realized that another messenger had arrived:

"Do you have a minute? I have a message from your son. He told me to tell you that you have to get into your life and live it. He says, 'Life is for living, not for regret. I am with you.'"

This message has enabled me to regenerate. Shortly before that, I told Dain Heer that I wanted him to take me all over the world with him, because I didn't know how to survive, but he replied:

"I'm not the source of your strength. You are!"

It wasn't easy, but I decided not to give up and see where all this could lead me and how it could look. Am I surprised? I am! The story is no longer just mine, but now belongs to the whole world when they see me or hear me talk.

One day I came to New York to visit my daughter, who was living in this energetic city on the East Coast. However, I stayed in the hotel for the first two days, because she was still moving in. I came directly from the airport to the reception at the hotel, where a smiling black man waited for me with the usual welcome words. Perhaps in a different situation I would not pay attention, but the badge with the name Ivan was simply looking up at me from his chest.

I did not believe it, so I asked him:

"Excuse me, what's your name?"

"Ivan," he replied.

Still completely confused, I started talking about my son to a stranger. On his face, the mask of kindness turned into grief:

"I'm terribly sorry about your loss, ma'am," he said, and with a special glitter in his eyes, added:

"Welcome to New York. Unfortunately, we currently don't have a room ready for you; please try a little later."

My daughter arrived a few minutes later and found me completely stunned in the foyer. While I was talking about this unusual encounter and incredible coincidence with names, she began to cry and said through tears:

"I also feel that he is here with us."

After a few hours, I returned to the hotel, but Ivan was no longer there. Another young man was waiting for me with a message.

"Ivan is not here, but he booked you the best suite in the hotel, for the same price as your smaller room."

At first sight, it may have seemed like a small thing, but it strengthened me and turned my sorrow into joy, because Ivan was appearing everywhere, sending signals in a variety of ways to show me that he was with me and taking care of me after all.

Once again, a year after his death, he sent me an unexpected message. My friend Ana went to Annsofi Nilson, a psychic medium in Sweden. And she didn't go there because of me. But when she arrived there, Annsofi said:

"A young man came and said that a woman suffers for her lost son.

"He was the lost son because he was experiencing his life in this way, he constantly sinned, and no one understood him. He felt lost among people and couldn't find his place in the world.

"He wants to tell his mother that he will give her strength and gentleness, and he prays for her to live her life happily because of the time they spent together. He is no longer a lost son because he is now in the light. The darkness he wore with himself during his lifetime on planet Earth is sheltered, and one day he will return as a stronger individual. He chose the role of a lost son and does not want his mother to suffer anymore because we all have our choices, although they are sometimes bizarre and stupid."

"Do you have anything else to tell your mom?" Annsofi asked.

"Tell her that I am very grateful to her because she has always been a kindness in my life."

He used the same words he had always used earlier in this reality. This sweet tone could always bewitch us.

Once, he wrote to me for Mother's Day:

"Mom, thank you, because you are always here for me; without you I would not succeed. You are my inspiration and my guide. I am grateful for everything you do for me, and I will never forget you. Your son Ivan loves you."

At that time, I went through life like a sleepwalker. I could not stay in my apartment, and that's why I started my travels around the world. The apartment was only used as a place for me to change my clothes and move on.

So, that's how the first year passed, in anger and rage because he left me, although he constantly said that we would be together when I grew old. I could not stand that feeling.

I cannot stand the term "good-bye" anymore; I always say:

"See you."

Once, my daughter and I had an argument in a restaurant because it seemed to her that I judged something important to her. Already annoyed, she said to me:

"I don't have any intention to sit here and receive this from you. Now I'll get up and go home."

"You'll leave me?", I screamed.

At this moment, my energy was rising like a volcano, because someone else was leaving me. Although she was already halfway out, energetic to leave the battlefield we'd just created, she felt something was wrong and returned. I was in complete distress, and my smart daughter "lowered the ball" and told me gently:

"Mom, you have to look at what's in your makeup that provokes such a reaction. How can I leave you? I'm your daughter, and you will never be left by me."

How much consciousness for one young being!

What can we do in a moment of rage?

At the moment you feel the rage, you should stop, draw the STOP sign in front of you, breathe deeply and exhale.

And say: Stop! What is this? How do I create this? Can I change this and how?

Or: Stop! What is this? Does this bring me pleasure and how? Stop! Who does this belongs to?

By placing these questions in your mind, the energy of anger is excluded, and when you say STOP, you stop this power. Energy starts to fade and has nowhere to go. This opens up new opportunities and new choices, where you can contribute to yourself and the people around you because the barriers go down and everything calms down.

I realized long ago that our loved ones are always with us. They may have lost the form we are accustomed to seeing, the physical form we love, but that's not all our love.

Our love is much deeper, it's universal, and there is no beginning, no end, no definition, no conclusion and no judgment. It's our love.

We cannot find loved beings in their material form, and we cannot communicate it the way that we are used to, but they are here. They haven't gone anywhere, and our connection hasn't been interrupted. It continues, only in a different form. Keep in mind that love is completely present, as you are at this moment. It's love that follows you everywhere and is not inseparable from your presence, love that whispers to you late into the night and wakes you in the morning.

"I AM HERE!" Love says.

Love asks you to adjust that which is without shape, to let her out of your dreams, and that you do not have to worry. Yes, you will feel incredible amounts of pain, a lot of sadness will appear, but with courage and readiness you will move on. Be prepared to leave your heart open for love and joy, discovering that your loved ones are here, next to you. Know that they have not left you and never will.

Separation doesn't exist. They are part of you, and you are part of them.

In fact, this connection never ends, it never disappears, nothing can interrupt it—neither death, nor divorce, nor termination. In reality, there are no two people who have ever broken up. It's just the story we've learned. We only "break up" with the old pictures that we have about each other, with our ideas about what we needed or what we could have been, with past and future hopes and plans, with our misconceptions and illusions, with dreams about the future that will never happen. We just end up with a story that no longer contributes to us. That is all. Our relationships, connections and life never really end—they evolve, change shape and form.

Love does not recognize space and time and cannot end, because it is the force that connects us all. What we are can never be divided or broken, destroyed.

The heart does not know death and separation. WE ARE ONE.

What if...

What would you do if you knew there was no division between anyone and anything on this planet?

What would you choose then?

What would you choose, if there was no judgment anymore?

Would you regret something you missed today?

Would you regret something you said?

Would you regret something you didn't say?

After the murder of my son, I made the most important choice of my life. I chose to live.

I chose life, here and now, despite everything. I chose to work and change what wasn't good for me. I chose not to sit and complain about what happened. Instead, I was active and tried in different ways to find something that would be my contribution. People criticized me terribly because of that. My mother said:

"Your son is dead, why should you live, why don't you kill yourself? Do you intend to live now?"

A close friend was very upset when I decided to celebrate my fiftieth birthday four months after my son's murder and went to Costa Rica. When I called her for a celebration, she said:

"Why should we come? What do you still have to live for? Your son is dead! What are you celebrating?"

And more:

"And how can you put your photos on Facebook ?! You should grieve!"

I understood her because we learned so, especially if you belong to a Christian religion. If you look at the history of the Balkans, in countries such as Serbia and Greece, the mother would have worn black clothes to prove her commitment to and regret over the child for the rest of her life. And that's still the case. My way of dealing with the death of a son and the regret for him was controversial for many. However, for many others, I became an inspiration.

Years later, I received messages from people who followed my posts on Facebook. For them, I was contributing to their lives during a situation that could not compare with what I went through, but I gave them hope that there is always a choice, that we are not alone. I have met and still meet mothers whose children use drugs. By sharing my own experiences, I give them great relief and support.

On the other hand, long after Ivan's death, I judged myself terribly. But somewhere in my Universe, I chose to live. I believed that Ivan didn't want me to die. He was a bigger contributor to me than I was aware of, even when I was not sure if I would be able to continue living. I felt as if some light led me through this terrible period and led me to proceed further.

Was Ivan that light? And how did I survive?

After his death, I spent a year on trainings, in solitude, and in retreat to let my body heal. I found a new way to be with myself in that system and make choices that were not even close to those I had chosen before.

First, I started to question myself. For example, I realized that I spent too much time with people who are negative and have destructive habits. I asked myself:

"Why do you spend time with them? What are you talking about? What are your thoughts when you're with them or afterwards?"

I realized that the initial gatherings with friends, with whom I spent time smoking and drinking wine and complaining about problems, were no longer my choice.

Secondly, I faced the memories that I kept alive and became aware of how they were creating my present life.

For your own situation:

1. Re-examine your habits.

2. Face the memories you keep in your life and discover what they are creating for you. If you continue to think and act in the same way as you did yesterday, without noticing what you are creating in your life, and if you do not try to choose something different from time to time, you will not be able to rid yourself of the control of the outside world.

Chapter *Seven*

Choosing joy and gratitude

One day you will wake up, and there won't be any
more time to do the things you've always wanted.
Do it now.

—PAULO COELHO

Are you looking for something outside of yourself to make you feel happy?

Nothing and nobody can really make you happy. You cannot make other people happy, and you cannot make them sad. It's actually just a choice.

How can I be sure that it is actually the case?

I spent a lot of time working with thousands of people and their stories are similar: "I'm trying to make my family happy, including my children, and I'm failing."

What is happiness?

People on our planet believe that unhappiness is more real than happiness, because more people feel unhappy. And true happiness is in peace and joy. Unhappiness is made to justify your dissatisfaction. You cannot actually be unhappy, if you do not work on it. It's a changeable state that you've produced, thinking that you have no control over it, and in fact you have complete control. Thoughts, feelings and emotions are a system of justification for everything in your life.

What do you share with other people when you are happy?

You have little to share. No one wants the thoughts, feelings and emotions of a happy person. Just think about how much time you spend with your friends talking about how happy you are and how good your life is, compared to how much time you have been talking about problems and things that you are not satisfied with.

If peace and joy were the usual state of being on this planet, would we have wars? Would we have therapy groups? These are all systems that are set up to maintain the existence of unhappiness and dissatisfaction. Without it, the world would fall apart. Unhappiness is the one thing that holds the world together in disrepair.

And in fact, the more you smile, the more you heal the world.

If you are happy, then you will transform the general state of the planet, and everything unpleasant that has happened in your past. And then you will not have anything to do!

Depression is a condition in which we choose the worst possible way, and more than anything else, we wish to express our unhappiness, because people want to show that they are the greatest in their misfortune. Therefore, depression is their choice, because many roads open then. If you are unhappy enough, then this condition allows you to take medications, go to therapy, go to church and pray. It allows you to do everything that is not considered "right" when you are happy. It provides you various justifications and even allows you to not work.

On the other hand, why are you looking for happiness outside of yourself? It does not work that way! If people or things that make you happy disappear from your environment or from your life, you will be unhappy. Therefore, you should create happiness in yourself, so that you can always be as happy as you are with those people or things. Can another person or some other thing really make you happy? Why would you give someone or something beyond you such power that it can affect whether you are happy or sad, instead of being the source of your own happiness?

Joy, calmness and opportunities create happiness.

How would you like to build your life?

You don't need anything when you choose to be happy. You don't need religions, temples, or churches, because for the happy person the whole Universe is a temple, the whole existence is a church.

What do I know about joy?

Who am I to talk about joy? Basically, I think I know both sides well. What is JOY? What does it mean for you? JOY is a sense of PEACE! Do you have a sense of peace? JOY is the source of life. Do you allow yourself to feel JOY in your body?

Happiness has nothing to do with ambition or success. It has nothing to do with money, power, or prestige. It's a completely different dimension. Happiness is associated with consciousness, not with character. If you don't think about what's going on in your life, if you don't think about the past, if you don't worry about the future, then it's impossible to be unhappy.

If you think someone has done something evil or not good for you, it's just your point of view. To perceive it as evil, you would have to be where it happened and have done it to yourself.

We "give" people far more power than ourselves. And nobody is more powerful than us. So, if you judge that someone is more powerful or worse, or anything like that, you need to "uncreate" and destroy everything you have been or done. When you realize that it was also you, or you did it, and that this is the only reason why you might have a problem with that situation, the problem suddenly disappears.

> *"Remember, if you don't create your own life, others will do it for you. This is your choice."*
> —GARY DOUGLAS

What did you choose to show that you are different?

What did you choose just because you could, without making any sense to anyone, to show how different you are? Did you experience unkindness or abuse and chose to be a kind person? Or, you grew up with little money and chose to change that? Or, you grew up with people who were constantly judging, and you chose to be above it?

Would you confirm that you made a different reality than the one you were given when you were a child? Is this sufficient proof of how rful you are? And will you admit that this is YOUR CHOICE, and not the education that created your life and the way you live?

When you wake up tomorrow, choose to be happy and stay happy. It's just a choice, there are no secrets. Just try it!

If you choose to be unhappy, nothing is wrong with it, that's your decision, but then just hold on to it. Stay unhappy no matter what happens. If you get a gift, or win a lottery and people adore you, do not worry, just stay unhappy. Even if you get the promotion, or your partner wants to marry you, or all your wishes are fulfilled, stay unhappy. It's also a choice.

But you can also choose to be happy. In your life there may be such choices that no one else can see and magic for which no one else is ready.

You have the capacity to choose what you want to be. Happy or unhappy? When you decide what you want and you become aware that this is your decision, then you become the master of your Universe and the opportunities that are opening up to you. And then there are no more excuses for giving someone else the power that can affect your happiness or sadness.

Once I read the inspirational story about Buddha, and I want to share it with you.

Buddha was passing through a village, and a few people on the street started insulting him. He listened carefully, filled with love. When they finished, he told them calmly:

"If you said everything you wanted to say, can I go now? I need to get to another village before sunset. If you still have something to tell me, I'll be back in a couple of days and then you can tell me everything you want."

The people were confused and asked him:

"Aren't you mad at us? We insulted you, said those malicious things."

Buddha replied completely calmly:

"You started too late. You should have done it ten years ago, and then you would be able to disturb me. Then I was not my own master. Now, it's your free will to offend me and my free will is to choose whether it affects me or not. I do not want to take it from you. What will you do with it?

In the last village I visited, people came with sweets, and I said that I did not need them, so they had to take them back. What do you think they did with the sweets?"

People looked at each other and offered:

"They must have shared them in the village, or they ate them by themselves."

Buddha again calmly said:

"Now think about you. You came with these insults and I say— enough. I'm done with this. What will you do with them? You'll have to take them back. I'm sorry about you. That's your decision. Life is your decision, your freedom."

When you make a choice, many opportunities appear

The only thing on this planet that does not change is your awareness or consciousness. That's it! Are you ready?

It starts with you. Simplicity, light, joy and the way to consciousness is not something that happens as a random event and then ends. No!

It starts and never stops! This is a continuous process. When you make a choice, there are many opportunities because you are willing to receive them. And there's no turning back. How will you remember the way back to the past if you face light and joy every day? Every day is so unique that there is no reason to go back. You will once again become a child, and there will be no limits to your growth and connection with the Earth, life and the Universe.

How did I choose the joy?

Many people ask me this in trainings. Did I choose it consciously, immediately, or how...?

There was always a desire to find out and discover something more. For more than twenty years, I studied various modalities and read everything I could find about the philosophy of life. I observed people, and at the same time watched myself, and my behavior. I realized that when I am more willing to observe and be more conscious, there is more joy. The more I meditate and I choose to be grateful for breathing, I can feel more JOY.

The more joy, the more flow.

The more I smile, the more quickly I move to the essence of my being.

One of my favorite writers, Osho says:

"Every way of life leads to death—the life of a poor man, the life of a rich man, the life of the unsuccessful, the life of the wise, the life of the sinner, and the life of the saint. Every way of life moves towards death. So, how can you be in love with life and live, if you are against death?"

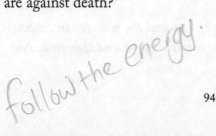
follow the energy

This sentence is constantly in my consciousness, and it follows me in every situation. The way my son was killed was, in my opinion, terrible, violent and not fair. His life was shortened and he was torn away from me. Is that right!? Why? I still have no answer—not even deeper understanding that would lead to answer the question.

When we are really aware, everything is turned on, and nothing is turned off. Consciousness can make you and keep you happy, but it can also make you unhappy and miserable. You can look at it as good and bad, or you can look at it from a place of acceptance that there is no answer. It's so simple.

What can I change now, and what kind of contribution can be made to others now?

The golden key is permissiveness

Being in contact with yourself and with your deeper state of consciousness will look like reluctance, if you do it through anger, greed, possessiveness, guilt, shame, or regret. The golden key is permissiveness. Nobody can replace my child. The wound stays; maybe it can never heal, but I have to go on. He is like the rose that gave me thirty years of its life. I have experienced his laughter, my joy, and my grief...and with his own creation, his mission is over. He returned to Source. It was his life, his choice.

That's an example of how consciousness found its way into my life. It showed me death, but I chose to flow like a river. I was frozen for some time, then melted and continued on. I chose to step into my bravery and live completely, intensely, dangerously, not to sacrifice because of what we've been taught. I could have killed myself, to become a martyr, but I did not.

In my meditations, I have come to the truth that we are here because of us, not for anyone else. There are endless possibilities in us. There are countless layers. How to identify yourself? With your mind, with your body, with your ideologies, ideals, or just with what you are? Life asks us to enjoy! Life demands living! To enlighten ourselves, to flow with what we create, until we choose to die. Death is powerless, if you choose life. There is no reason why we would wait for it.

At trainings I meet a lot of people who are afraid to live. They are afraid of everything: because they will grow old, because they will live alone, they are afraid of cancer. And they are waiting. But there is nothing to wait for! Release it! You can live, or you can die. I chose LIFE! I do not believe in death. We do not die. It's just the energy that is given to us through the body, and then we move to another form.

Be grateful for your life

Be grateful for the life you chose. My mentor Gary Douglas says: "Gratitude is something we learn with the goal—to be grateful for what's happening to us! You need to find a place where, regardless of what's happening in your life, you will find consciousness. And if you are grateful for this consciousness, your gratitude will expand and grow, and your consciousness and money will flow as electricity into your life, and the prosperity in your body."

That's so true.

Twenty years ago I was introduced to homeopathy for the first time, and after that I visited my homeopath, my good friend Andreas Kalderon, once a month. From the start I was asked to practice gratitude.

He said: "On the day when you become grateful for everything—for the good, for the bad, for the evil, for your parents, for everything you have or you are—your life will change."

At that time, I did not know what that meant. Today, I ask you to practice observation from a distance, every day. There is a huge potential for gratitude there. Our words create. Our thoughts create. There are vibrations in our words. Whatever happens in your life, you can get awareness about the possibilities of receiving. Whenever you meet someone, ask yourself how can you be grateful for that?

If we live in judging, we reject everything and everyone in our lives. Gratitude, on the other hand, strengthens our relations, increases happiness and the good of our entire being. Remember, judgment and gratitude cannot exist in the same Universe.

What if the gratitude of people in our lives can extend both our and their lives?

Chapter Eight

Choosing to take risks and never give up

You may not realize it when it happens, but a kick in the teeth may be the best thing in the world for you.

—WALT DISNEY

The first company founded by Walt Disney went bankrupt. Instead of giving up, he went to Hollywood with one suitcase and twenty dollars in his pocket to start a new business. He believed in himself and his ideas, and nothing could stop him. It turns out he was right.

Michael Jordan was kicked out of the basketball team in the second year of college because he was too short. But he continued to play and became one of the best in the world.

Winston Churchill was a bad student, and he was punished many times as a result. He also had a speech impediment. Churchill became the Prime Minister of the United Kingdom and a Nobel laureate.

These people, and others like them, teach us that we need to believe in ourselves and sometimes take extreme risks in order to create an amazing life. And that we need to stick to our dreams and ideas, even when everybody around us "sends messages" that we cannot achieve it. Some people walk long and hard steps toward what they want, while others walk slowly.

It does not matter what category you belong to as long as you are ready to take a risk for your ideas. It may sometimes happen that you jump towards your target, because the moment presents itself, rather than exercise or meditate about it for days, weeks, months, or even years. Hesitation can lead to missed opportunities that occur only once in a lifetime. Just use logic and make sure to take necessary precautions and protect yourself.

If something is blocking you…

If you feel that you are ready to take more risks, but something is blocking you, and you feel stuck, find the root of the problem. You might be feeling fear, or have limiting beliefs about the risks. Perhaps you do not even know what stops you from taking the risk or what the risk is that you should take. You may just feel that every time you want to get out of your comfort zone and try something new—you freeze and dig in even further. This is a perfect opportunity to review your beliefs about risks, failures and mistakes. Also, in this way, you can become aware of your beliefs and thoughts about yourself and your abilities.

A person can take a risk and make a mistake, but it is not a failure until he or she decides how to experience it. Are you worried about what other people will think about you? How to measure success? Are you afraid of success? Do you suffer from a lack of self-confidence and self-esteem? Negative and restrictive beliefs in some, or in all of these areas, have to be eradicated, re-engineered, and replaced by positive beliefs so you can start moving forward. It is time to ask questions without expecting mandatory answers to them, and different possibilities will appear in your life.

A human being has a huge amount of energy, and the more energy you use, the more you will get. If you have a stressful situation, don't "fight" with your body. Instead, ask the question: *What is needed here?*

It may happen that you feel stressed, but, what if it's not stress? What if it's the way your body is dealing with a particular situation or challenge?

ENJOY the challenge.

It is very important that you believe in yourself and take risks. Keeping the mind full of positive beliefs will support, encourage and push you forward. When you start to risk, amazing things will start to happen—an amazing life will take place, and at its center there will be an amazing person. You are that incredible person!

Do you know that energy never dies?

Why do we believe that we are dying? Why do we give up on ourselves? These are the questions I asked myself every time I wanted to die or go to bed and never wake up again. Perhaps you are surprised that I write this, but these moments have appeared in my life many times. I realized that we do it to tell ourselves that we have no choice and that we never chose to be here. This means that we can always blame someone else for the bad things that we create.

Who are we cheating by doing this? Someone else or ourselves?

The key is to understand that we are beings with choices.

One of the choices is to start to risk and never give up.

So, how did I practice taking risks and not giving up?

When I opened my own company in 2010, I had no idea how it would work. Working in the corporate world for more than 20 years, with money secure in my bank account every month, did not provide me with any experience on how to reorient myself into a different business environment that would allow me to create.

Well, the choice creates consciousness, which, in turn, creates a greater choice and more awareness, but you need to start somewhere. And I did. I wrote my marketing and action plan, but I had no idea how to make it all happen. I wrote that my vision is to contribute to people to reach their full potential and take steps towards their abilities and skills. I wrote that I would be working all over the world and that one day I would be a guest on Oprah Winfrey, where I would inspire people to free themselves from fear.

What seemed impossible has become possible! I sold the apartment and went to Italy for the class "Energetic Synthesis of Being (ESB)" with Dr. Dain Heer. My journey continued to Croatia, although I didn't know anybody there. I went out of curiosity and held my first workshop with only four people in an apartment.

Three years later, more than a hundred people came to listen to my lecture "Letting Go by Living NOW."

It was as if I was suddenly riding on a wave of possibilities, and new things appeared in my life. I asked questions. And I changed...

I stopped seeing friends who did not support my new path and was in complete allowance of my choices without judging those in my personal Universe. I laughed at my mistakes by spending money on opening up a market that previously did not exist.

"One day, everyone will come to you. Just keep going, and everything will come back to you," my mentor Gary Douglas told me.

At the same time, I knew that I had myself, and that I would always have myself, and that's why I wanted to make the most of who I was. The more I asked, the more opportunities opened for me and I felt complete freedom. My life began to flow like a mountain river; I gave and gave more. I became all: power, joy, passion, motivation, sensuality, seduction...and I allowed myself to play with all the possible ways of being I enjoyed.

Do you know that you can live by energy?

I used the Access Consciousness tools and discovered more and more the beauty of energy. Do you know that you can live by energy? It is everywhere. How often do you allow it to come into your body? Right now, pull energy into your body from everything that surrounds you. Pull more! How does it feel? Are you ready to allow your body to feed, live and simply exist?

I was not thinking about the money. I spent everything I had on trips, with one single goal—to create and experience. The world accepted me. Wonderful people, my sisters and brothers. It seemed that everyone wanted to be on my side and to contribute.

Every place on planet Earth has something that can contribute to us, heal us and enable us to become one with consciousness.

I risked everything for my freedom, and I put everything that I had towards living the joy that was possible. Here, is where I found life going on for me. I lived as a traveler for years, once again discovering myself. My inner child returned to me, the passion of life returned, no longer just to survive, but to progress.

My accountant said:

"You spend all the money you earn on travel. This is a very expensive hobby. This isn't the way you develop a business."

I laughed out loud. My laughter crossed the hills and valleys, when she said that. Who cares!!! I AM ALIVE!!!

This is a gift I received from my son.

Before the trial of my son's killers, Gary Douglas called to give me the strength to be able to go through what was to follow. He told me this incredible statement, which confused me at first:

"Everything is the opposite of what it appears to be, and nothing is the opposite of what it appears to be." (Later when I became 3-day Body Class Facilitator I learned this is the Body Process method of Access Consciousness that is used when you have problems with insomnia, or when you are overly "in your head.")

He repeated that for ten minutes after which we could talk about Ivan from a different perspective:

"What if your son could not contribute to the world and to you while he was in the physical body, but now he will be able to? You just have to ask him. You can talk to him. He's here with you. Where would he like to be and make his contribution? Do you think that this is perhaps your opportunity to travel the world and expand consciousness?"

I said yes! And yes!

YES, my son is a great contributor to me. Every day! His suffering inspires people to choose something else. His story brings people to my classes. His energy is in every class and through this, he lives.

Chapter *Nine*

Choosing to ask questions

The journey of a thousand miles begins with one step.
—LAO TZU

We are all transforming into something else. Today, after nine years, this is completely clear to me because the Universe or God has confirmed it to me in many ways. We all return to the Universe, we are here with a reason and people in our lives that are of our own creation. Today, as a coach, I recommend to my students to consider who surrounds them in their lives and everything else that is their external reality, and to feel the reaction each causes within them. And then to simply ask questions.

The questions will open up opportunities and show you the choices that are available. The questions will give you an awareness of the

ation. The questions can create peace, and the answers will give
awareness.

I've used these extremely precious questions when I get stuck on
anything and am not sure how to proceed. I just ask:

1. *What is this?*

2. *What can I do with it?*

3. *Can I change it?*

4. *If I can, how can I do it?*

Ask questions, and don't try to *find* the answers; let them come to
you. Does that seem unusual? It doesn't matter. Just keep asking
these questions. When you *try* to find meaning in something or to
understand, then you are dragging your energy, asking it to adjust
and agree, or to give resistance, or have a reaction. When this
type of aligning or reworking is done as "work," then you deprive
yourself of the ability to stand aside and, without judging, look at
the situation as an observer. So, when you ask questions, just look
at a certain situation as it is in the present, and don't judge or try
to manipulate the responses that come to you.

Please continue to ask these four questions until you get full
clarity about what the situation is. Your logical mind does not
have to understand it. It's about changing its energy, and for you,
stepping into the source where you'll see a wider picture. When
you step out of the trauma and drama of what you call your life, it
will also change for other people. And they will reject the creation
of drama and trauma in their own lives.

Living life in question

Living life in question is much more than putting the question mark at the end of a sentence. This is a way to transform such that you "become" the question. Many of your current answers prevent you from feeling joy, bliss and unity. When we live "in question," without trying to find the answer, we allow the Universe to give us a response that is greater than we could have found on our own. When you begin to live life in question, it all starts to appear as though magically. The more you ask questions, the more aware you become of the opportunities you have.

In the beginning, I asked questions in a way that implied a certain outcome. This isn't how it works, so I couldn't feel the energy of what I was doing. So I decided to ask questions just for fun. For example, I wondered, "What could I create now just for fun? Where would I like to go?"

I created an energy bowl in which I placed a piece of paper to bring energy for my life. It was really without any strategy and plan. I wrote on the paper that I would like to travel around the world and give people the tools I have, so that they can access their knowledge. I wrote that I would like to "produce" more than ten thousand euros a month, to have wonderful friends, discover beautiful places, make a world-class business and co-create with people all over the world. In addition, I would like to live in love and tenderness, in nurturing relationships, traveling with the love of my life all over the world—to enjoy life. I was ready to do whatever it takes to change the drama and trauma of my life to joy and celebration. After I did this, I continued to ask questions every day, ready to follow the signals that surfaced.

Prior to this, I was used to abusing myself and living life with constant difficulties and struggles and it took some time to get out of these patterns. Nothing would change in the moment.

I dragged the dread and unrecognizable despair with me as a suitcase full of personal things.

Today, I still don't remember the first year after Ivan's death. The second year was confusing, full of sorrow, anger, regret, and guilt. I wanted justice, and this experience was painful for me because I had the feeling that I had gotten something completely different. And this created a double pain.

Buddha explained this:

"There are two arrows that hit us. The first is an initial event, a painful experience. It happened; it cannot be returned. The second arrow is the one we turn to ourselves. This arrow is optional. We can add anger, stiffness, and fear to the initial pain. Or, we can learn to experience the same painful event with less identification and repulsion, with the relaxation and grace of the heart."

It's my way!

My way is to be in a state of complete relaxation, to live in trust, to respect myself, to remain in a condition of gratitude and allowance, no matter what happens and how it appears. I realized that anger and bitterness are not our true condition. That's not what we are. In a state of allowance, when we are asking—what this means for us—and in a state of our own change, everything around us will begin to change. This is what we need to develop, to return to our capacities, our true strengths and kindnesses.

Yes, it can be a difficult job! But, yes, it's worth it!

Every day I started with these sentences:

All of life comes to me with ease, joy and glory!®

What energy, space and consciousness can I be in order to be filled with kindness, inner strength and joy?

I was determined to do whatever it took just to gather the courage to live!

Who are you?

Many people in my workshops ask: "Who am I?"

Do not ever ask that question. Instead, ask every day: "What contribution can I be on planet Earth?"

With this question, everything in your life will begin to change. It's not about who we are. It's about what we are willing to contribute and receive. There's nothing to fix. Our only job is to live and make progress.

Here are some of the questions that I have asked in the past few years:

- Where is my energy needed? Where is my contribution required? What contribution can I be to the world today? What contribution is the world for me?

- What energy, space and consciousness can I and my body be in to create a desired life, with absolute ease?

- What energy, space and consciousness can I be in to re-create my body every day?

Here are some more questions you can ask yourself every day:

- What energy, space and consciousness can I and my body be in such that I always believe in myself for all time?

- What energy, space and consciousness can I and my body be in to feel completely safe alone and never need anyone for all time?

Why should you choose to ask these questions?

If you want to live like most people on this planet, you don't need these tools. But if you want to live in your way, then use your energy to raise your life to a higher level.

All that you resist and what you perceive as negative will turn your energy against you to keep you stuck and potentially destroy your life.

When you need something, you make it more important than yourself. When you don't need anything, you are completely free; you are not tied to anybody or anything that you believe you cannot live without. When you do not need anything or anyone, you are free from fear that someone can leave you. It's the greatest power you can have.

If the Universe is in you, do you need anything or anyone?

Do you know that the greatest strength is in gratitude, kindness, generosity of the spirit, freedom from need and solitude, because these allow you to be all you really are, without anything or anyone who has power over you?

Would you like to be the master of your life?

Ask: What does consciousness require of me every morning? What energy space and consciousness can me and my body be in to be grateful for me?

There is only one true evil in the world—that is unconsciousness.

Everything else is a creation.

You are the creator and source of your strength.

You can create a completely different life.

The choice is yours.

PART IV

Coaching and Meditations

Coaching

In my story and in Ivan's story, I have indicated how the tools I use in the workshops I teach have come into play in my own life. Following are some simple explanations and manifestations of these tools. Some may matter to you, some may not mean much right now. But as you become aware, they will start to make sense, and you will see their impact in your own lives as well. By sharing these "coaching sessions" with you here, I hope to provide another mechanism for you to tap into the positive energies around you and make different choices in life.

The magic of consciousness

Today, through many techniques, and by science (from Nikola Tesla to quantum physics), we know that "magic" is embedded in our consciousness and that it is not as mystical as we think. Unconsciousness is a conclusion; the magic lies within true consciousness. When we tap into the magic that exists all around us, we transition into a state that allows us to truly receive it. When we are aware, we perceive, are, know and receive everything including the thoughts, feelings and emotions of others. To some, it is a magical gift, to others, it is "enlightenment."

What does it mean to function consciously?

It means to be aware of what we think and what we say. You have to become aware of what you're saying and thinking, so that you don't create what you don't want. What if you created your life as you desire? If you live your whole life without justification, reason, judgment and beliefs, it will all happen very easily. What if you were not what you have defined yourself as, but merely space?

Ultimate freedom lies in knowing that awareness is just a way of living consciously. It is not right or wrong, good or bad. It is just noticing.

If you are ready to have that consciousness, and you want to fully feel it in your body, then you are actually part of the present. You are experiencing it all as gifting and receiving at the same time. But that does not mean that you do not have to do anything about it. That's why it's good to keep on wondering: Is this about right now? Or is it about the future? How can I use this awareness to my advantage?

Through my lectures and training I discovered that when people become aware of how and what they choose; for example, if they become angry, sad, or have other difficulties, this is a choice. Then, they can make different choices, or if this seems too difficult, ask for a different choice. Upon "getting" this information, they become completely relaxed and receive gifts from one another, entering, at that moment, into the capacity of their true nature.

Conflict lines

Our parents played the most important role in our development, positive and negative, and strong negative traits continue to affect our ability to form relationships and experience success.

My conflict line turned out to be when I was ten and my parents left me and went to Austria, and I did not understand why.

After that, I saw Ivan's death as leaving, and again I did not understand why. All other relations took place between these two important links, important conflict lines.

My reaction to "leaving" was terrible anger and rage, until I realized that was my choice. And I could choose something. I could choose joy.

The powerlessness of money

Growing up, I'd been told repeatedly by my parents that we had no money. Mother was constantly saving, mostly on her own. She bought me the most expensive clothes, but she never respected herself. This continued until the day of her departure from this reality. Even when she was losing her memory, she was intent on instilling in me the need for money. This was her way of showing her love. At the same time, she never wished to receive any gifts from me.

It was the same with my father. Even today, with a house, a car and a secure retirement, he says, "I'm a social case." In our Universe, there was never any money. I've never heard, "Wow, we have money, what will we do with this money?"

When you grow up in such an environment, it becomes your reality.

That's why I decided to change my points of view about money by working with other people who had a different perspective. And then teach others the tools.

My first workshop was in Zagreb, Croatia. Just a few hours before the workshop I fell incredibly ill. Nausea, vomiting, headache. However, I did not cancel the workshop.

My first question for the group: "What does money mean to you?"

The answers were emotional: "I am sick of it, I have no power, my head hurts to think about it, I have to fight for it, freedom, security, it does not exist in our country..." There was a lot to let loose. Then I realized how my sensitivity was operating. I captured this energy before the workshop started, and I processed it through my consciousness, thinking it was mine. And I made myself ill.

Isn't that interesting—what the power of collective consciousness can create?

My second question was: "What do you mean to money?"

The answers were: "Nothing, pain, sorrow, I do not know, fights..."

I also asked some other questions, such as: "How do you feel about money? What emotions do you have about money? If money were a person, who would it be...?"

The group brought forth different ideas, views, emotions and feelings, which I received. And I experienced a miracle. The more I facilitated them to release their fears and preconceived notions, the better I felt physically. By the end of the workshop, my symptoms were gone.

We are not fully aware of our own power—how the thoughts and emotions of others can be made our own, even energetically. Our negative thinking, our stubborn points of view, create constraints and

25

parameters that limit what we can receive. It's rare for us to function from a place of abundance that is already within us. We usually seek it from the outside. It's rare for us to be connected to one another and every creature at this level, with each molecule that supports a different level of energy and power. After this workshop, I realized that abundance creates our strength, awareness, creativity and control. We are life; we are energy. And abundance, too, is nothing more than energy.

Where did we pick up a lie that the money is something outside of us?

We are unlimited energy, and every time we choose the consciousness that is aligned with the energy of abundance, we stand in our creativity and our strength, and we can change our physical reality. That day, I decided that I would personally change my energy to align with abundance. Every time I found myself thinking that I did not have something, or that I was in error, or that I lacked, I chose to release these thoughts from their origin, until I could create a new space around me. Then I would ask myself:

What do I love to see being created on planet Earth?

What do I desire in my physical reality?

Where is my contribution needed?

What can I create and generate with total ease and joy?

How can I receive more money than I can spend?

When we connect with the vision and the power of what we want to accomplish, we follow that energy and allow the Universe to show us the way and deliver what we want.

Money in and of itself is not important. What is important is what you wish to create in your time here on this planet. Money is the by-product. If you are willing to be the power of you and the change in the world, money will come as a result of that. What do you want to accomplish? My truth and my desire are to continue to express myself, to

116

ask for awareness in every area of my life, and in this way to allow the Universe to give me the chances and opportunities that I am grateful for. What is your truth?

Try this exercise for 30 days!

Every morning say this phrase to yourself 10 times:

I am POWER! I am CREATIVITY! I am JOY! I am MONEY! I am CONSCIOUSNESS!

Saving yourself

Today I know that we must never lose ourselves. But how can a child have known that? And how can we help it when the world does us wrong?

We always have to ask ourselves what the truth is and what the lie is. It's easy to distinguish them. The truth is always light and easy, and the lie is difficult. When we accept patterns as our reality, just because we are used to them, the conclusions we reach cause us to slowly lose ourselves, our true nature.

Some people are so sensitive that it's painful for them to look at what's happening around them. They get out of their body and only observe, and the body becomes numb to life. Have you ever noticed people's eyes? Have you noticed that some people are just watching and walking without a smile, without life; it is just the body there? The soul is gone, and there is no one inside. This happens when we think it's too painful to live here and do not accept our capacities and strength.

What is anger?

As a child, were you allowed to get angry when you had an opinion or point of view about something, or were you silenced? Have you been allowed to step into your power when you ask for something to be delivered to you? Probably not, and you interpreted it as an anger. When it is really power!

When someone wants to control you, then pushes their energy at you, this is anger. Anger is the energy you can transform to stand in your capacity. Here's how:

If you get angry, just stop. Put a visual sign STOP in front of you. Breathe and exhale. Lower all barriers down, and allow energy to flow through you. When you do, you will feel expanded, and at the same time, everything will be easier. Just have the will to do that.

When you "get into your strength", people misinterpret this as anger, and you "buy their screenings" that it is true. And you give up that energy.

I learned that anger is an implant of interference with which other people control us, and we do the same to others.

Do you ever wonder what is "under" anger? Is that yours? The question and tool I used to change that energy is:

What invention do I use for the anger I choose? Am I willing to let it go?

YES!

Projections and expectations

Projections and expectations are what others (and you) believe that your life should look like. And not just this one. These are the projections we carry from other lives. We take them with us as a worn suitcase. How many projections have others installed on you—how to behave; and how many of the truths or lies that were "sold" to you have you "bought"? And when you did not manage to meet the expectations of others, then you "went inward" and separated from yourself. Where did this lead you? It led you to refusal and separation from your true Being.

Growing up, I had to be good, and I never managed to stand in a different energy. I was true evil to myself, so that I could prove to others that I was good. My projection was that I should see my son marry, to be a grandmother, and that they live in that one marriage my entire life. That is the order in which life should go, that's what we imagine life should look like.

Where is the awareness? Where is the perspective of life? How many of you have accepted the program that you need to worry about others, or what will people say? What will others think about you? How much vibration do you enter only to get someone to love and accept you based on their terms, and what does this do to you? It locks you into the reality of a lie that creates a slight destruction of life, little by little, as you slowly move away from yourself.

If this resonates, ask the questions:

What kind of expectations do I have of myself?

And what else is possible?

Have you decided that something must be the way you have imagined? That's your conclusion. Every time you accept that something "must be" and "should be," you have destroyed other opportunities. Your only job is to look at what projections you have accepted and what projections and expectations about yourself you have created.

Your point of view creates your reality. Your projections and expectations are the secret points of view about you and are created from your perspective. And in this way you have reduced yourself and your awareness to that one perspective. But what if that perspective doesn't suit you? How will you know?

It helped me to wonder and ask myself every day—how to get into something much bigger and much better. What are the infinite possibilities today? What would it take for today to be greater than yesterday?

Does that mean I'm always in the mood?

NO! Sometimes I'm angry, sometimes crying, sometimes nervous, but that's only for a moment, and then I choose a different feeling. I ask myself questions every day.

Every day I do something that will serve to create my life tomorrow.

In this way, I always get out of projections and expectations, and I enter into creation.

Do you have a projection that you are unsuccessful? What do you think will show up in your life? Failure, of course.

Would you be willing to dismiss it now? Only by being aware of it, you can choose differently. I've learned something else that I will share with you—I never stop, no matter what happens.

I'm going further, I choose more...

YOU ARE THE POWER

How do we defend ourselves against fear?

According to American psychologist Will Schutz, the founder of FIRO Theory (Fundamental Interpersonal Relations Orientation), we all want to be important, special and loved. When we do not feel this, we enter "defense mode," which we don't recognize because we don't have consciousness of ourselves. From this fear comes rigidity and control. We all have fear that somebody will ignore, humiliate or reject us. And these feelings create our behavior.

My mother was not seen by my father, at least not in the way she wanted, and therefore she was defending herself with rudeness and insensitivity, but essentially she wasn't that kind of person. We want others to see us in our own way, the way we imagine ourselves, and if not, we just lock all the doors to people.

When I studied and later practiced and began to teach what I had learned about this theory, I realized at what point in my own life I stopped listening and hearing, because at that moment I closed my consciousness. This is the state we enter when we think that we are the only ones who are right. And only when we become aware of it, can we choose something else and change the energy.

Our reality consists of our thoughts, which, like interwoven strings, pass through our mind. Our experience plays a big role in how we see life and how we relate to others. It creates our joy or our despair, especially in communication with other people. If you have grown up in a family where interactions are constantly on the verge of breaking, you can experience the world as an un-secure and unpredictable place, even if your current reality is safe and supportive.

And, how can we get out of this?

- *Do not carry into the future what has blocked you in the past. Manage your own self-confidence. Use meditation and other tools to become aware of your fears, values, intentions, and other feelings;*

become the master of your future, not the victim of your past. Self-consciousness is the first step and the biggest initiator of change.

- *Appreciate and respect others.*

- *Recognize there are other attitudes and reactions; be flexible in your responses to others.*

At workshops, I like to teach people how to let go of the past, re-create the future and feel their own power. Many people carry the past in front of themselves as a knight shield, when, in fact, it is just a decayed suitcase that causes us problems in relationships with others.

How many of you are trying to hide or avoid the fear that comes with taking risks in your life? When you become ready to open your eyes, you will free the energy that keeps you trapped to the past, and transform it into life and joy.

Learning to choose

Each of us experiences a situation in our own way. It was the same with my parents. They often expressed their behavior through anger, which became their mode of domination, and which, even if they were not aware of it, was destroying their lives. Many people saw their behavior as power. I tried to understand them, but instead of doing so, I have become an angry person myself. At the time, I was not aware that one of my capacities was to contribute to other people. I just wanted to fit in, so I copied my mom and my father, took on their behavior patterns, without knowing that I had the ability to change it.

Nobody teaches us that we have a choice.

Everyone tells us what's good for us and we make choices—based on the answers we get from others:

Imagine if your parents asked you:

"What would you choose today?"

"What do you know about this situation?"

"What do you think about that? What is your point of view?"

And they do not judge your answers.

Would that make a difference?

Today I know that I have a choice and that I always did—and that I will not make a mistake whatever I choose. I know how strong I am because of my choices and because, by asking questions, I always have different options to choose.

When I ask people at training sessions about their choices, usually three or four answers appear—and that's it. There are more options if we just let ourselves explore the possibilities.

Nobody teaches us how to make choices.

So, what are we doing? Just copying.

Do not continue to copy the patterns and responses of others. Change it up!

Learn to make your own choices and be proud of them.

Responsibility for our reality

When I was 17, I married and created with my husband the same relationship that my parents had.

Isn't that interesting? All that I was running away from was waiting for me on the other side, and it became my reality again!

Is this reality our choice?

Are we the ones responsible for it?

Can we choose something different?

Why you wouldn't you choose to be truly loved then? It's your birthright!

Why life isn't just fun?

Why is everything so difficult? Why are problems constantly arising?

Because we are not taking responsibility for our own reality and surrendering to outside forces we believe have all the control.

When do we become conscious?

Consciousness is achieved through different experiences, which are neither good nor bad. These are just our roles in different movies. When we come to live a life in which we only contribute, we come to understand the choices that have not served us in the past, and we know now that we will not choose those again in this life. When we realize how it "works," when we become aware of it, then we live with ease.

I became aware of that when I realized that something was wrong in my life. That's why I want to share with others that if they feel similarly, they can change.

The release of judgment

Judgment is always heavy energy. When we judge something, then we get into difficulty, because judgment is always a lie. All the evaluations we have about the world—good or bad, right or wrong, keep us from becoming ONE. Our viewpoint, right or wrong, good or bad, comes from a conditioned mind, and it needs to be freed.

Every moment is just as it is. Nothing is good or bad, right or wrong.

When we look at things and occasions in this way, we become free.

To judge something as good or bad means that we do not believe there is a greater intelligence in the Universe, and that everything is just a coincidence. Even if we believe that occurrences happen randomly, if we believe the opinions and judgments of our mind, this keeps us trapped in our thoughts, and often trapped in suffering.

Judgment creates a deep gap and separates us from what we have on our minds and what the target of our evaluation is.

Some of the questions recommended in Access Consciousness:

Would an infinite being really choose this?

And if an infinite being did not choose this, why did you?

Is it necessary for an infinite being to judge?

Is it necessary for an omniscient being to judge?

Is it necessary for the final being to judge?

Should a person who " knows" judge?

Therefore, judgment is the absolute denial of infinite existence and of us as the infinite beings that we truly are.

If some part of our life doesn't function well, it is because we justify it, explain it, judge it, or believe it. Every time we judge, we stop the energy of creation and create the energy of destruction.

If we give people the freedom to choose, they will begin to recognize what is best for them, and they will be fully aware of what they need to do.

Be aware. Do not be unconscious, take drugs—do not take drugs.

It's only your choice. You choose. Like with everything else.

In any case—without judgment.

My parents were constantly in the "who is right" mood? And that means you're never free. But, the more empowered I become, the more I choose to be free. What did I manage to create in the past when I chose to be right? What did I create with that during my marriage?

I created:

- *the pain*
- *suffering*
- *financial problems*
- *dramatic connections*
- *control*
- *living out of feelings, thoughts, and emotions. (Emotions are an important part of our being. If we let them pass like a cloud, they cannot control us. But if we give them importance, then they will take control of us.)*
- *dealing with problems*
- *the need to push energy (So, if someone doesn't want to go in the direction that I want, then I will push because I want to be right.)*

What could I do? And what can you do? Lower the barriers and look from the viewpoint of another person, become wiser. Then you won't need to be right anymore.

Full permission is the key to empowerment

Choose one part of your body. What do you think of it? Judge! Now, do not judge your opinion, that first judgment. Do you feel different?

The only judgment you need to accept is that you can change it. The greatest freedom is to try new points of view that you have about everything. About every person you meet, about every situation—everything is just the way it is. Without judgment.

People usually think that decisions, judgments and conclusions are the sources of creation. You need to decide, conclude and judge, to determine what you will create. If you live your life from energy, space and consciousness, then you have a different attitude. You do not have one judgment that is defining you.

Consciousness is created by choices, not by judgments.

Oneness includes everything, judging nothing, and, as a result, there are infinite choices and infinite possibilities.

Everything is a choice. Everything is infinite possibility. Everything is the question, nothing is the answer. Be the source of your strength, and the world will change.

The choice is your real creation.

Functioning from sorrow, pain and suffering

So, I know what it means when you live out of sorrow, pain and suffering. I was born and was walking on that road where rage, frustration, fear, sadness, suspicion, and addiction were everyday companions. We live in a program that keeps us stuck in projections, expectations, judgments, separations and rejection from all others and, of course, from ourselves.

In order to be able to get out of this program, so that you can maintain the correctness of this reality, you cut up the pieces of your consciousness. I know I was doing that. Why? I was looking for ways to do the right thing.

But this is not a solution.

The solution is to choose the awareness.

Why do you refuse to receive consciousness?

Have you tried drugs? Have you tested your body? Maybe by food, alcohol, medication, exercise, sex...? What is it that you refuse to be, see, know, and receive about yourself so that you suppress your thoughts, feelings and emotions, believing that it will release you from them?

What is it that prevents you from choosing consciousness as information? Why do you refuse to receive consciousness?

You do not have to do anything with it. You can only receive information.

Living from joy

Are you too sensitive? Or your child? Or your spouse? Or someone you know?

This does not mean that something is wrong with you; it can be a huge capacity! Highly sensitive persons feel intensely—happiness, joy, pain, and sorrow, and the great influence of other people's moods and emotions; they are deeply touched by music or art. Often they are bothered by loud music, voices, and noise.

What if you can enjoy it?

What if everything is fine with you? Would you be willing to change your perspective on this?

It is our reality to suppress feelings and take medication when we are hypersensitive. If we have a headache, we take a pill instead of going out into nature to breathe. It is the same with drugs. We take them with the intention of reducing our sensitivity and experiencing superficial joy instead of real joy.

One evening I went to my favorite bar. A man invited me to drink a glass of champagne with him, but I refused, explaining that I was driving.

"That can't be a reason," he scolded. "How can you go out on a Friday night and not drink when everyone around you is drinking? How can you endure?"

His point of view indicates that we must drink if we want be part of the masses, and not separate ourselves from other people. That's what we learn at a young age, when we first start socializing in public places. And then we take medicines to reduce consciousness, emotions, reduce the energy of people around us and the disturbing impact they can have on us.

My experience with thousands of people says that if you have the right tools, you can actually direct this sensitivity in another direction and turn it into your advantage.

If you live from joy, bliss, and ecstasy in life, medications and drugs are not necessary. You will have endless possibilities, and you will be able to access all of your capacities, talents and abilities.

What do we create?

When I became so sick that I couldn't walk, when I was giving and taking care of everyone except myself, when I was tied to my bed for six weeks and the doctors thought I was paralyzed—in this process I lost the meaning of life and existence. The desire to be greater than life had completely disappeared, and everything was about doing something right, to fit into this reality, to evaluate other people and their points of view more than me and my point of view. I forgot who I was.

Please, do not do what I did! Don't go that way! It's not a good choice!

How much freedom did I allow myself by creating such a life? And what about what I got? Where did it go? I did not see that I could choose something different, and I concluded that life is just like that— you have to fight and work hard.

We have conclusions in life based on our society, cults and religions, and so on, which tell us what we can do or be, as long as we work in a certain, acceptable way. We think that somewhere, someone knows the right answer.

But there is no solution in the answers, because the answers are always conclusions. They limit us as to what we already see and prevent us from going on.

My dear friends, nothing is wrong with you! You are not born in sin. You were not destined for a bunch of spiritual garbage. Your life is not missing anything essential. Others try to convince you that you are not good enough, because they feel so. In your innocence, and without evidence that says the opposite, you believe it. So you spent all those years of your life, trying to fix it, cleanse and perfect yourself.

Just like me.

I lived in two kinds of worlds—a business one, where I met people who functioned in a different way and behaved differently than the other world of my parents and family. Later, with the tools I learned, I could see what was happening around me. It became easier, and my point of view changed.

The meditations that follow can help you to discover new points of view to help you see through your own creations to find the joy and connection.

Meditation is a gift to yourself

Once you have tasted meditation, it is impossible for you to be in any misery. Bliss becomes inevitable.
—OSHO

What is meditation? Meditation means gifting yourself a few moments when you are not in your mind—a few moments when you let go of your mind and slip into what is!

When I studied Kundalini Yoga my teacher, Gurmukh, used to say:

"We have to start sometime and somewhere to get to what we are asking for and to change. Sometime could be now. And somewhere is where we are at this moment. Start now! There is no tomorrow, and nothing to wait for."

Meditation is the tool for getting in touch with what is really going on inside of us. I am not saying that we have to sit in a position for hours. Meditation can occur when you wash the dishes, when you walk in the woods, when you eat an orange. When I studied yoga, we were asked to eat a piece of fruit for one hour. Touch it, be with it, taste it, look at it, don't rush. Meditation can be asking questions and not going into answers or results. Meditation can be expanding in all directions 100,000 miles and connecting with the Earth. There are so many techniques for how to "do" it. In this book you have a sampling of tools and practices that can start to change things for you.

What is beyond the flow of thoughts that initially clutter our inner terrain? One of the things I have discovered is that I can feel happy and sad at the same time. I can be happy, angry, upset, laughing, extroverted, introverted—all of this can be going on simultaneously. Fear and excitement can be there at the same time—why is it like this?

Isn't life and the Universe within all of us, which means that we have choice at every moment? The question here is: Where would I like to put my attention, and which reality do I wish to choose? With the tools of Access Consciousness I learned the tool of how to live in 10-second increments.

What if you had only 10 seconds to live the rest of your life?

If you lived your life from these 10 seconds, as though there were no more, what would you really choose?

I used the questions below to find awareness. There were so many decisions and judgments in my world that I have bought, which were the lies running me.

Please try this yourself. Run this process for 30 days, every day, 30 times per day. Write down your answers.

1. What have I created that is so valuable in this life, that if I don't have it, I'll have no reason to live?

2. What am I unwilling to lose, that if I lost it, it would take away my life?

3. What am I holding on to with such intensity that I would destroy my body rather than let it go?

I remember when I did my teacher's training and my task was to get up every morning at 4 a.m. for six weeks and do one hour of yoga and one hour of meditation before taking a cold shower and rubbing my body with almond oil.

Was it nice?

Not always, but I did for 21 days in a row, and I felt amazing. This is how I began my programs for changing different areas of my life. This is my secret! I dedicated myself to doing it no matter what, just to experience what it could create for me.

When I began studying the tools of Access Consciousness, Gary Douglas used to say:

"Run this process and question 30 times per day for 365 days."

It took me years to get what he was saying. Yes, we have to practice to change something, but we will always find reasons and justifications for not choosing to create and stepping into our capacites.

One day I decided that nothing was going to stop me from finding me. And you can too.

Allow yourself to get in touch with the fear, the impatience, the anger, the sadness—all the emotions coming up for you and ask yourself:

Is this really relevant to me? For what reason? Is it mine? Who does this belong to?

Continue to ask these questions during your meditation.

Whenever the mind starts this type of chatter ask:

Who does this belong to?

When we reach a space where we are in allowance of all energies and acknowledge that none of them belong to us, we are on our way to finding freedom.

We are accessing the being, the peace, the joy and the infinite possibilities.

The meditations here are for you to choose a different possibility. To let go of the past, stop thinking of the future and drop out of time so that you can live your life fully in the present.

Play with them! Choose them in 10-second increments.

Meditation for being alive and living fully

Not only do you have to be willing to lose your constructs and utopian ideals, you also have to be willing to lose your convictions and points of view.

    Once you are willing to lose everything, new possibilities will show up for you. You will be unfettered by limitation.

—**GARY DOUGLAS**

1. Take a piece of paper, and on that paper draw ten rectangles to represent suitcases. Take a moment, and think of people that you love and that have significance in your life. Write a name on each suitcase. It can be your parents, children, friends, lovers, colleagues.... Put the ones that you can let go of immediately in the last row, and the ones that mean the

135

most to you in the first row. Think of those boxes as suitcases with memories that have followed you in this life and other lifetimes.

2. Sit comfortably, close your eyes, and take a few deep, relaxing breaths. Relax your shoulders. Feel your breath. As you become aware of the space around you, let go of your everyday thoughts, and put attention on your breath. Feel how your body relaxes and how you have a sense of peace and calm within.

3. Picture yourself as a little baby coming into this world with your ten suitcases. You are in a limousine, you are taken care of, and everybody adores you. You are the center of the world—loved, cared for, cuddled with, and laughing. Your smallest gesture is appreciated, and you are traveling in the limo arriving in a new city.

4. The journey into this city has come to its end, and you have to let go of four suitcases. Say goodbye to them. Tell them that you love them and you are grateful for the experiences you have had together with no point of view on whether it was good or bad. Let go of all grudges of the past or present. Just release and forgive. Put your hands on your heart. Bring your attention to your body. Tell your heart and your body that you are taken care of, and everything is fine. Connect with the Universe, and pull energy from the Universe through your body and down to the Earth. Connect with the earth—with the water, plants, animals and trees. Say goodbye to the limousine, and now go to the train station. You are going to take the train.

5. You are travelling, having fun, enjoying, meeting new people, and you have your six suitcases with you. They are there to support you. You are smiling. Embrace all the possibilities coming towards you. Imagine colors around you. There is no rush. Life is not in a hurry. Be like the seasons. Winter is

not trying to become summer. Spring does not rush towards autumn. The grass grows at its own pace. We can be more like that. Connect with the plants, animals, trees and the planet.

6. The train is at the last station. Now it is time to let go of four more suitcases because the rest of the journey is on a motorbike, and you have space for only two suitcases. Do the same procedures as in step number 4 above to release them and move on. Do not look back. Look forward on the road. Move fast and have more fun.

7. You are at the end of the road. You can't drive here. You are only allowed to walk in nature by foot. You have to let go of one more suitcase. Do the same procedure as before. It may be a little bit harder for you. The two suitcases left are full of emotions, but you have to choose. Remember that you will see them again. This is just for now, and you have to go on. This is what you have committed to. Now walk on the road and move forward. Look at all the beauty around you. You are in, greeting animals, trees, flowers, and they are all there to support you. Enjoy, breathe, and see the colors of beauty that are around and within you. Everything is here to support you.

8. You have come to a mountain, and you have to climb to the top. You have to say goodbye to the last suitcase. Stay here as long as you need. Open your heart. Allow yourself to be vulnerable. Just relax and embrace the mystery of life, sink deeply into the moment, and then, perhaps without effort and struggle, the answers will come, emerging and giving you what you are asking for.

9. Climb the mountain. You are now on the top of the mountain. Stand up. Raise your hands to the sky. Allow the energy from the Universe to flow through your hands, into your heart, through your heart, down to your belly, your hips, legs, toes

and down into the Earth. Pull energy through to the Earth, your entire body and into your heart.

10. Expand that energy all over and now connect with every person that you have been in contact with through all lifetimes. Connect with every single plant, flower, tree, mountain, and ocean, and be one with them. Let that energy move through you and your entire body. Express your gratitude! More! More! More! More! More! More! More!

This is YOU! You are not alone! You have never been alone! You are everything! You are the source! You are JOY! You are the flame that never dies!

This "journey" demonstrates that when we free ourselves of attachments, we are truly free. When we live with the sense that something is missing, we are not fulfilled. To be truly free in the heart, we have to let our attachments to others go. By setting them free, we can set ourselves free.

Meditation for choosing joy

JOY arises within; it has nothing to do with the outside. It is not caused by others; it is not caused at all. It is the spontaneous flow of your own energy.

Joy has to be shared. By sharing it, you are unburdened. By sharing it, new sources open up within you, new streams, and new springs. That sharing of your JOY IS LOVE.

—OSHO

Every morning when you wake up, you have two choices. You can choose to be in a good mood, or you can choose to be in a bad mood. Each time something bad happens, you can choose to be a victim, or you can choose to turn it into your advantage. It doesn't matter what you have chosen in the past or what is going on; what matters is—what are you going to choose now?

Changing your point of view means being willing to be and do something different. The joy of choice is that you have the ability to change your mind *every 10 seconds*. Would you consider living your life in 10-second increments? What would your choice be in each of those 10 seconds? When I ask this question in my workshops, most people only see two or three potential choices, and they've already decided what those are.

This meditation will open you up to many more choices, things you may never have considered. There are always more choices!

Start your morning by repeating several times:

What energy space and consciousness can I and my body be in to receive this day in a greater and easier way than I ever could have imagined and and destroy and uncreate everything that doesn't allow me to receive that?

Take a couple of minutes in bed to stretch your body, touch your body and express gratitude for you body.

You have all choices possible.

The ones that create limitation and the ones that create expansion. The ones that create grief and the ones that create JOY.

What if we receive the contribution we are on Earth by every choice we make? Would that create a different possibility? Our energy is what creates! What energy are you willing to be?

1. Sit comfortably, close your eyes, and take a few deep, relaxing breaths. Relax your shoulders. Feel your breath. As you become aware of the space around you, let go of your everyday thoughts, and put attention on your breath. Feel how your body relaxes, and you have a sense of peace and calm within.

Take a deep breath in from the top of your head and down to your toes and into the Earth. And again…exhale through your whole sweet body and out through your feet. Do it again!

Imagine a time in your life when you were joyful. A beautiful moment of JOY. Feel the details of that moment. Imagine happy, joyful people, playing, having gratitude for each other. Tap into the energy of the way it would be to have your life and living be everything you hoped for and know it could be.

Ask to connect with that energy. Connect with the plants, the trees and the animals. Pull energy from Universe in front of you, around you, the same energy that circulates around the Earth.

2. Perceive your body, your breath; be aware of what is going on around you. Perceive the space you are in. Connect with the four corners of the room, and imagine yourself occupying the room. Expand and take the space of the city or town you live in…and expand.

3. Concentrate on your crown chakra, and imagine golden light vibrating.

Say to yourself out loud: I am power, I am creativity, I am JOY, I am the light of my Soul.

You are the beauty of this world in a human body. Ask your body to release and unlock the unhappiness. Move your hands in front of you and on 3, let it go. 1-2-3!

Imagine receiving from the Devas, Spirits and Angels. Imagine receiving from everywhere. Allow the abundant Universe to contribute to you.

4. Move your attention to your third eye, in the middle of your eyebrows. Imagine the sun and moon embracing each other—the sun in gold and the moon in silver. Allow that light to expand in front of you like a highway that is crystal clear.

Repeat: I am power, I am creativity, I am JOY, I am the light of my soul. I´m here, and nothing can stop me. I´ll make everything greater. I am the gift to a possible world that has JOY and EASE.

5. Move your attention to your heart. Imagine a blue light and a star shining.

Repeat: I am power, I am creativity, I am JOY, and I am the light of my soul.

Connect with the Earth. Imagine yourself as the being of Light and acknowledge that you are here to contribute to a greater change on Planet Earth.

6. Move your attention to your solar plexus. Put your left hand on your thymus (below your neck) and your right on your solar plexus (below your rib cage). Feel the heat from your hands.

Feel your hands on your body. Feel your body in your hands. Connect with the plants, animals, trees, water and Earth. Allow yourself to expand even more. The Universe is within you! You are the Universe!

Repeat: I am power, I am creativity, I am JOY, I am the light of my soul.

Connect with the Earth. Pull more energy and allow that energy to connect with ever molecule that dance and play in space. This is your capacity, your ability, your potency. This is who you BE!

Something that I practiced for a long time was to meditate on death. Who is dying? Is it the body or the being? Or is it so that we never die!? We just change form! From the physical form to formless or another form that we are not able to see with our limited minds.

Have you watched your thoughts sometimes? At night when you fall asleep? The last thought, the last desire, the last fragment of your mind?

If you were thinking of someone you love, or a situation that bothers you, or whatever is going on for you...that is the first thing in the morning that will come to you.

The last thought of this life will be the first thought of another life.

A very useful tool is to destroy and uncreate everything.

All your relationships, your creations, everything! Just destroy and uncreate it! Say it! 10 times!

Meditate for 5 minutes. Just lay down on your bed, and close your eyes. Put your hands on your belly. Ask your body to relax by taking a couple of deep breaths.

See yourself disappearing!

See how the world looks when you are gone.

Think: One day I will be gone. I'll be dead. This body is going to take a rest and transform. Life will go on. The radio will go on. People will go on. Without you, and with you in another form, everything will continue.

Think: I have no more reality! I am not!

Let go!

Good night! Rest!

In the morning when you wake up, take a moment. Put your hands on your face. Express your gratitude for your body and for a new morning. Start to laugh! Laugh! Laugh! For a couple of minutes and then ask 10 times:

What energy, space and consciousness can I and my body be in to create today greater than yesterday?

This will bring the JOY back! Welcome LIFE!

Meditation for making a choice

Vladica, you have the gift to always move forward!
Don't let anything stop you from what you can be,
do, have, create and generate.

—DAIN HEER

This meditation can be done for a few minutes to start, and then gradually continue up to 31 minutes.

1. Sit in an easy pose with a straight spine or in a chair. Put your hands in a prayer position. You can also put your left hand on your heart and your right hand over your left hand. Take a deep breath. Exhale. Do it again.

    Be with your breath. Allow yourself to relax so that you breathe with the frequency of your body. Observe your thoughts and your feelings.

    Ask: What am I thinking? What thought dominates my space? Who does this belong to? Bring your attention to that.

What am I feeling? Is this mine? Something else or somebody else's? Ask that question a few times.

2. Raise your arms, and with your arms raised, take a couple of deep breaths. Imagine a target, something that you would love to achieve. It may be a great relationship, success in your business, losing weight, quitting smoking, bringing peace to the Earth, or whatever it might be for you.

3. Start with moving your arms as if you are swimming. Extend one arm and the other in a constant motion. As you swim imagine yourself in a vast ocean as night is falling and a storm is coming. You cannot see the shore, so use your intuition to determine which way to go to reach the shore. Project yourself in whatever direction your intuition takes you. Imagine, your survival depends on swimming in the correct direction. Swim vigorously so the motion will automatically give you the rhythm of breath you need to survive.

4. Let go of the thoughts of fear. Focus on the shore. Imagine everything in the ocean is willing to contribute to you, giving you the energy to carry on. Nothing can STOP YOU! NOTHING! Not even YOU: You know where you are going. You know why you are here. You know how to get to the shore with ease, joy and glory. Imagine yourself and the gift you are to the world. Imagine the beauty of the world and the contribution you are. Ask for that energy to move through your body.

5. You are getting closer. The light is bigger. Put a smile on your face and show your face that you are happy, strong, persistent and potent, and you are the leader, in charge of your path of awareness and consciousness.

Allow everything that comes during the meditation to come up and continue. The light is brighter, and it is getting closer. People are on the shore waiting for you to contribute to you. You are not alone, beautiful you.

6. You are on the shore! Inhale deeply, and bow with your head to the Earth. Be still there for a while in a child's pose and move the spine in all directions to loosen it up. Let the spine readjust itself. Express your gratitude to the Earth for greeting you. Gradually, rise up and relax your shoulders. Put your hands on your heart and express your gratitude to your beautiful body assisting you here.

7. Open up your eyes and greet all the beautiful people waiting to greet you with flowers, joy and gifts.

YOU ARE THE BEAUTIFUL GIFT TO THE WORLD!

YES, YOU! YOU ARE HERE, BORN TO CONTRIBUTE AND STEP INTO ALL THE CAPACITIES YOU POSSESS!

Please be happy, respect happiness, honor happiness and help people to choose happiness. It is as natural to be joyous as it is to be healthy. We are one with life, and it goes on, moving! Everybody is breathing, and everybody is unique. Life goes on every day singing a new song and painting a new creation. Every moment. Please start where you are! By changing yourself, you will change the world. Let us help each other to learn a totally new language! Only if we do that, can we change the face of humanity!

Meditation for gratitude

*Let us rise up and be thankful, for if we didn't learn
a lot today, at least we learned a little. And if we
didn't learn a little, at least we didn't get sick, and
if we get sick, at least we didn't die, so let us be
thankful.*

—GAUTAMA BUDDHA

The book begins with gratitude, and it ends with gratitude.

WHY?

If you allow yourself to receive from the bad, ugly, good, right, and
wrong, there is nothing in the world that can hurt you, kill you,
or destroy you.

Only YOU!

This meditation is from my own experience and a great tool to contribute to receiving your body. I start the morning by expressing gratitude to my body for my choices, for my life, and then I ask questions, bringing gratitude to the present moment, and I am aware of the energy it creates.

My body is working, my heart, my liver, my kidneys and my eyes. I am alive!

Scientists have documented the social, physical and psychological benefits of gratitude. I am not a scientist. I am an energy worker, a light worker, and I have my own science that tells me it works! I empower people to know what they know. I know that gratitude increases your happiness and invites greater satisfaction in your relationships. It softens your heart and invites receiving.

1. Sit in an easy pose with a straight spine or in a chair or lie down on a yoga mat or in your bed. Take a deep breath from the top of your head down to your toes. Put your left hand on your chest and the right on your solar plexus thanking you for being here, for the beautiful you that you are on planet Earth. Thank your sweet body for the gift it is. Thank You for the possibilities and awareness that you are.

2. Continue to breathe gently. Be with your breath for a couple of minutes.

3. Take a deep breath again, and as you let it out, be aware of the Earth, the nature and the beauty as it is. Connect with the energy of the Earth. The energy that you can receive is regenerative for you and your body. What information does Earth have for you? What gifting, what kindness, what awareness of you and the sparkle of life and living? What is available for us? What is Earth, our home, contributing to us?

149

What would it take for us to have a sustainable living here where we contribute to the planet and the planet to us?

4. Continue to breathe gently. Bring to mind someone you care about, someone it is easy to rejoice for. Picture them and feel the natural joy you have for their well-being, for their happiness and success. With each breath, offer them your grateful, heartfelt wishes. Ask these questions in silence:

5. What can we be and do to create and generate together today what will make this day and beyond phenomenal?

6. What would it be like if the gift we are to each other can be received with no judgment?

7. Open up your heart and send trickles of energy to that person's heart.

Say THANK YOU! THANK YOU! THANK YOU! I am so grateful for having you in my life.

May you be joyful.

May your happiness increase.

May everything you desire in your life come into fruition.

What contribution can I be to you?

8. Allow your awareness to expand in all directions, including down into the Earth; occupy a space of 10 miles in all directions. Allow yourself to expand even more so that you occupy 100 miles, and allow it to embrace you and enfold you in loving and caring arms. Allow it to contribute to your body and to the planet.

9. Allow it to embrace and show you the brilliance of you in totality.

10. Allow yourself to expand even more and be connected with the Earth where you are contributing to each other. Be aware of your body and how you breathe and allow yourself to expand even more, including down into the Earth. Ask Earth to gift to you the awareness and the communion it knows is possible.

11. Allow yourself to be with the vibration of the Earth. Connect with your knowing. What do you know about you? Expand even more, 1,000 miles in all directions and out into the cosmos. Allow all the molecules to cling together. Allow any amount of energy to contribute to you and contribute simultaneously to the Earth.

12. Continue to be in that space. Open the meditation to include all people on the planet, your friends, your enemies, your relatives; connect with beings everywhere, young and old, near and far.

13. Say THANK YOU! THANK YOU! THANK YOU! I am so grateful for having you in my life.

    May you be joyful.

    May your happiness increase.

    May everything you desire in your life come into fruition.

    What contribution can I be to you? What contribution can we be to each other? What contribution can we be to the Earth?

14. Open up your heart even more and allow trickles of energy to simultaneously give and receive and be with everything.

15. Take a deep breath in again from the top of your head and down to your toes. Thank your beautiful body for being such an amazing gift. Thank your body for gifting you an awareness of what is possible!

16. Thank you for being such a gift to you and everyone around you, whether they acknowledge it or not. The plants, the trees, the wind, the animals, the surface you are laying on right now—what if you are the consciousness and in oneness with everything?

17. Take another deep breath in from the top your head and down to your toes. Wiggle your fingers and your toes and allow your body to know that you are here.

    Open up YOUR eyes slowly. THANK YOU! THANK YOU! THANK YOU!

This is a way to lower the barriers so that we are not separate, so that we all can be together in Oneness and receive. What if you allow your heart and body to resonate with the planet and let awareness open up?

Imagine that you are allowing yourself to surrender to space—the space that will gift to you continuously.

What if the purpose of life is to have more fun? NOW IS THE TIME!!!

Take another deep breath in from the top of your head and down to your toes. Wiggle your fingers and your toes, and allow your body to know that you are here.

Thank YOU! Thank YOU! Thank YOU!

Lightning Source UK Ltd.
Milton Keynes UK
UKHW041017310320
361121UK00001B/78